Advance Praise for

Industrial Evolution

Lyle Estill conveys the insight and breadth of a true visionary
with the plain-spoken, common sense of your favorite uncle.
Likewise, *Industrial Evolution* shows how the key to the very
survival of our civilization lies in the rational, incremental return
of commerce and innovation to the realm of the real-world,
human-scaled community. This is the path.

— Douglas Rushkoff, author of *Life Inc: How Corporatism
Conquered the World and How We Can Take it Back*

Industrial Evolution is a report from the front lines of the
sustainability movement, conveying both its promise and its
frustrations. Estill is a reliable guide, and anyone interested
in the future should find his story riveting.

— Richard Heinberg, Senior Fellow, Post Carbon Institute,
and author, *Peak Everything*

Lyle Estill tells the amazing story of how a biofuel company
became, among other things, a worm ranch, a garlic farm,
a housing coop, and a foundation. In short, *Industrial Evolution*
reveals how a vibrant business created a resilient community,
able to ride out the credit crunch, Depression 2.0, and whatever
else that's thrown at the folks at Piedmont Biofuels.

— Novella Carpenter, author of
Farm City: The Education of an Urban Farmer

Industrial Evolution

Local Solutions for
a Low Carbon Future

LYLE ESTILL

NEW SOCIETY PUBLISHERS

Cover design by Diane McIntosh. Oil drums © iStock (aki yoko);
Sunflowers © iStock (Photographer Olympus, matejmm)
Interior photos Tami Schwerin

Printed in Canada. First printing April 2011.

Paperback ISBN: 978-0-86571-674-2
eISBN: 978-1-55092-480-0

Inquiries regarding requests to reprint all or part of *Industrial Evolution* should
be addressed to New Society Publishers at the address below.

To order directly from the publishers, please call toll-free (North America)
1-800-567-6772, or order online at www.newsociety.com

Any other inquiries can be directed by mail to:
New Society Publishers
P.O. Box 189, Gabriola Island, BC V0R 1X0, Canada
(250) 247-9737

Library and Archives Canada Cataloguing in Publication
Estill, Lyle
Industrial evolution : local solutions for a low carbon future / Lyle Estill.
Includes bibliographical references and index.
ISBN 978-0-86571-674-2

1. Small business--Environmental aspects. 2. Entrepreneurship--
Environmental aspects. 3. Sustainable development--Environmental
aspects. 4. Environmental economics. I. Title.

HD2341.E87 2011   658.02'2   C2011-900867-X

New Society Publishers' mission is to publish books that contribute in fundamental
ways to building an ecologically sustainable and just society, and to do so with
the least possible impact on the environment, in a manner that models this
vision. We are committed to doing this not just through education, but through
action. Our printed, bound books are printed on Forest Stewardship Council-
certified acid-free paper that is **100% post-consumer recycled** (100% old
growth forest-free), processed chlorine free, and printed with vegetable-based,
low-VOC inks, with covers produced using FSC-certified stock. New Society
also works to reduce its carbon footprint, and purchases carbon offsets based on
an annual audit to ensure a carbon neutral footprint. For further information,
or to browse our full list of books and purchase securely, visit our website at:
www.newsociety.com

NEW SOCIETY PUBLISHERS

MIX
Paper from
responsible sources
FSC
www.fsc.org
FSC® C016245

Contents

To my brother Jim,
who may be skeptical of me and my stories
but who loves and respects me just the same.

Acknowledgments

I'VE NOTICED THAT the "Acknowledgments" section of my books is getting longer over the years. It could be that I am becoming increasingly indebted, thereby needing more space for "thank-yous," or perhaps I am learning better to share my gratitude.

Whatever the case, I need to thank Tami and the boys for suffering through yet another book. It could be they like leaving town so that I can have the kitchen table in peace, but I secretly hope they wish I could tag along on their many adventures.

Tami needs standalone recognition. She's not only a great speller, she reads with a sharp eye, and more importantly, she coasts through her husband's angst and writerly horrors with ease and aplomb.

And I would like to thank my daughters Jessalyn and Kaitlin for being sounding boards and for offering feedback on some of my ideas. Jessalyn continues to remind me of my many "flops," and Kaitlin tends to offer a healthy skepticism for everything I do. I'd also like to acknowledge their mother Megan, who suffered through my early years of "wanting to be a writer," but who never got to experience the pain of when it "came true."

I also need to mention my brothers Glen and Jim, whose stalwart support has kept me going through the very dark days that followed the death of our brother Mark. Decades ago, when I had dropped out of school to write short stories, my brother Mark took me in so that I could try my hand at writing a novel. His only requirement was that I "work all day, every day." And I did that. I suppose I should also be grateful to the mice in our attic that have done a great service to literature by using those early manuscripts as nesting materials.

My parents, Ann and Don, belong high on the list. I should thank Mom for offering me her typewriter as a toy for me to play with in elementary school. And for her deep love of reading and rigorous intellect. And I should thank Dad for consistently giving me the courage to try things, even when they fail. He always used to say, "You're young. If it doesn't work out you can always do something different." He doesn't say that so much anymore, but that's OK. One of these days one of my ideas is going to hit it big, Dad. Honest.

And of course I need to thank the people of Piedmont Biofuels, and everyone else associated with our project. I don't dare name them all for fear of leaving an important person out, but these stories would not be possible without the hard work and dedication of everyone — from interns gone by to former employees and tenants, to those who have stood beside me in a grueling quest to find a "different way of being."

I do need to specifically thank those who have shared desks next to mine in our Control Room. That would include Piedmont co-founders Rachel Burton and Leif Forer; the creator of our design-build business David Thornton; and the creator of our Research and Analytics arm, Greg Austic. And I would be remiss if I forgot to include the sheer delight I derive from my working relationship with Chris Jude and Nick Fox, both of whom perpetually annoy me by wasting my precious time with the "facts." I've also greatly enjoyed the company, ideas, and performance of both Spencer and Amanda, who try to keep their desks far from mine in order to get their work done.

I must also thank John Breckenridge for his sage wisdom and advice, and Fran Hamilton for the same thing, plus her skilled massages. And I would like to thank Betsy Breckenridge for allowing me to use her splendid house on Topsail Island where I could work to the rhythm of waves, rather than the sound of children screaming over their Wii conquests.

I also need to thank my readers, who have criticized, fed back, complimented, and cheered over the years. I think of John Ousterhout, who occasionally vents, often comments thoughtfully, and sometimes merely corrects my thinking. And I think of those readers of Energy Blog that have posted, and railed and sometimes cheered for the ideas I have published there. To that end I need to pay special thanks to Ingrid Witvoet for not only leaving her island of Gabriola and making the trek to Pittsboro, but also for pulverizing ideas with me and encouraging me to write even when the struggle was evident.

I'm grateful to Bob and Camille Armantrout and everyone who attends Thursday Night Potluck at our bend in the Moncure Road. Bob and Camille arrived in our community thinking it would be a good place to weather the impending collapse of society, and they have become esteemed elders and dear friends along the way.

Of course I need to thank those dedicated and downtrodden workers in the "policy layer" — from grant-makers to scientific advisors to law-makers — who have taken the time to wrap their heads around our project and support us in various and sundry ways. Special thanks go to Larry Shirley, who is now North Carolina's "Green Jobs Czar," for inspiring us to keep the faith, and to Steven Burke at the North Carolina Biofuels Center for his patience, understanding, and commitment to the biofuels endeavor.

Finally, I thank our customers, which include everyone from Coop members who drive around on our artisanal fuel, to eaters who consume our sustainably produced food, to those who buy our co-products, to oil companies who buy our biodiesel. I am especially grateful to Brian Potter of Potter Oil for sustaining a vision of biodiesel in North Carolina and for including us in his journey.

Introduction

"**I**NDUSTRY" IS A FUNNY WORD. Sometimes it is a compliment. Think of the honeybee, which we generally hold in high esteem for its "industrious" nature. And sometimes it is an insult. After all, it is "industry" that pollutes the river.

I am an accidental "captain of industry," which I suppose makes me a cross between the virtuous honeybee and the evil polluter. I circle the word "industrial" like a hyena approaching a carcass — not sure if the lions are done feeding.

I once went to a weekend retreat that was staged by the good people of a popular environmental magazine. Everyone said they offered the best environmental writing in the country. I'd never heard of them. And I don't really care for retreats. But they had recently featured my friend Matt Rudolf in their magazine, and he was driving to the coast, and Bob and Camille were riding along so I reluctantly jumped in.

It was a beautiful fall weekend in North Carolina. The soybeans were still drying in the fields and the tundra swans were starting to arrive from Canada. I had just come from a meeting with Wes Jackson and Wendell Berry who had convened a group to discuss the formation of a "Fifty Year Farm Bill" for then-presidential candidate Obama.

The weekend guests were primarily self-absorbed "activists" and writers who could barely wait to read their latest poem or tome. They were swapping tales of how they strapped themselves to concrete barricades in order to stop heavy equipment from rolling. I sat quietly. I routinely order the services of bulldozers. I listened to their heroic stories of how they used activism to effect societal change. And I decided that I am not an activist. I use heavy equipment to clear weed species and trash from the woods so that another acre of sustainable produce can be put into cultivation, or so that a barn can be built.

Whenever I clear land in North Carolina I get criticized for destroying the forest. After the objectors have wandered off, I set about picking up the shards of plastic and glass and the vast amounts of metal that clutter our forests. I have never found the woods to be virgin. They have always been trashed by previous generations. At my house in Chatham County I can tell you about the previous owner's heart medication, and drinking habits, shoe

Kimberli Matin's brushed aluminum "Pond Scene" adorns the hill above the plant.

size, and favorite snack foods. After eighteen years of concerted effort, I still have garbage piles I haven't yet approached.

On my retreat weekend I strolled along a marshy boardwalk with one of the author hosts. In her poems she wrote about the winds on the Outer Banks of North Carolina, where she lived. I asked her opinion of harnessing those winds for electricity production and I explained that I was in the wind business in Canada with my brothers.

She said, "Not industrial scale wind I hope."

Drat. I was at odds again. It is "industrial" scale wind. My brother Glen has built 13 turbines in two discrete parts of Ontario, and each one is 1.6 megawatts or better. They have 40-meter blades, require a big gust to get them started, and they are beautiful when they are spinning. Hold the protest for a moment: we need to harness wind energy if we are to sustain human life on this remarkable planet.

In North Carolina, wind is something we write poems about. Not something we use to power our economy. And guys like me, who invest in "big wind," are suspect at writers' retreats.

It made me reflect on vocabulary. "Industrial" is synonymous with pollution, environmental racism, corporatism, war, and all that is wrong with the world.

That's too bad for me. I'm not an activist. I'm an industrialist.

I work at Piedmont Biofuels. That's a grassroots sustainability project that started in my backyard, became a cooperative fuel-making venture, and ended up as a community scale biodiesel plant. Our project sprawls across an abandoned industrial park that is currently home to over a dozen discrete, like-minded businesses ranging from hydroponics lettuce, to biopesticides, to sustainable produce, to worm castings.

For a long time everyone on our project referred to our little biodiesel plant as "the Coop," and to our "big" biodiesel plant as "Industrial."

"Industrial" was the place with the stage for live music, the playground, the giant chess set in the yard, and the place where people gathered for soccer night. In our town, Industrial is where you might be headed for lunch, or to pick up a box of sustainable produce, or to attend a Pecha Kucha presentation.

For many of us, industrial is an honorific term.

By now the boilers have largely been extinguished on the industrial age in America. Most of our manufacturing has moved away. But "industry" is a term that I would like to reclaim. Industry can evolve. It doesn't have to look like the industry of our fathers. Ants are industrious. People can be industrious. And industry can be a good thing. Ours is an industrious project.

On one occasion I gave a tour to Pamela Bell, who was one of the founders of Kate Spade. Unlike me she really *is* a captain of industry, with an intimate knowledge of the textile trade, outsourcing, and global commerce. We finished our tour and pulled up a couple of rocking chairs overlooking Piedmont Biofarm. She has an insatiable appetite for business ideas, and she was smitten with our little eco-industrial park. She's the one who coined the phrase "Industrial Evolution" as the title for this book.

"Evolution" is something I know considerably less about. My friend Michael Tiemann once hosted an international meeting of the Open Source Initiative in Pittsboro, where our plant is located. Some of his guests were stranded in an air traffic tangle in New York, and he was unable to start his meeting. To kill some time he brought those who had arrived for an impromptu tour. I led them around for an hour or so, and when I was done, he suggested that most people have misinterpreted the work of Charles Darwin.

"People sum it up as survival of the fittest," he said, "but really *On the Origin of Species* is about adaptation." He then went on to explain how Piedmont Biofuels had been forced to adapt time and again to shifting trends in the global marketplace, and to ever-changing government policy that is not quite sure what role biodiesel will play in America's fuel mix.

In the end, I'm just a storyteller. The stories I tell are the ones I have lived, which makes me sometimes wonder if I should shift to fiction so that I could suffer less. My first two books have occasionally inspired others to start projects or take action on changing their worlds.

I think of Megan, who started the farmers market at the marina in Lion's Head, Ontario. And of Tammy who threw in the towel on her rat race life in Atlanta to create an asparagus farm in Southern Pines, North Carolina. I think of Cole, who after a day at our park with his elementary school insisted that his parents allow him to plant peanuts in their backyard. And I think of the many small-scale biodiesel projects we have inspired along the way.

In my travels, both on the Internet and in 3D, I have learned that we have many people cheering for us, and hoping our project will succeed. As such I frequently find myself conflicted when I'm asked, "How can we replicate that here?" Whether I'm on stage as a speaker, or on the net, or simply having lunch, it's a question I can't easily answer.

I *don't* have a specific system, or a plan, or a solution. But I *do* have some stories to tell…

Breaking into the Business

WE TURNED ON OUR BIODIESEL PLANT in the fall of 2006. It sort of sputtered to life. We would make some fuel, then screw up some oil, then make some fuel, then throw a batch away. And by the time we had the hang of it the weather had grown cold. Cold is not your friend in the world of biodiesel.

So we adjusted our plant, and tweaked the process, and putzed around through the winter and by the spring of 2007 we were ready to make some fuel.

Chris Jude was at the helm. He singlehandedly kicked out forty thousand gallons of fuel, and for the first time in my biodiesel life I had a sales problem. I'd been making fuel since 2002 and never had enough to go around. When our plant began to spin like a top, our terminal filled up and I needed to get busy.

Sales problems don't scare me. I've been a traveling salesman for most of my adult life, and I thought it would be fun to move some fuel. So I visited almost every petroleum company in the Research Triangle Park region of North Carolina.

Petroleum enters the world in a strange and complex way. I had a sense of it from Lisa Margonelli's book, *Oil on the Brain,* in which she starts at a convenience store in California, and attempts to follow it back to its source. I entered the tangle just above the gas station level, at those firms who are delivering fuel "to the street."

On the distribution side, small family-run oil distributors have what are called "bulk plants," from which they fill most gas

Chris Jude, Piedmont's first intern, went on to drive our early production efforts.

stations. They typically have a large investment in trucks and tankage, and they are essentially in the logistics business.

Everyone buys from the "rack," where petroleum enters the state, and from there it finds its way through an octopus of trucks and tanks and dispensers. In North Carolina, petroleum fuel enters primarily from two pipelines that terminate in Charlotte and Greensboro, and begin in Louisiana. (We have limited coastal offloading capability as well.) Which means that when a hurricane slams into Louisiana, North Carolina runs out of fuel.

When I arrived at the door of the petroleum marketers I was generally treated as a curiosity. Almost all of them have the same story. It begins with "My granddaddy got a short truck and started hauling fuel for the..." and "My Daddy built up the business..." and so on.

Today, family-owned petroleum distribution companies are in a quandary. Most of them are too profitable to abandon, and too entrenched to sell. Many of them have been grandfathered into new environmental regulations that would prohibit their existence today; the installation of an underground tank today is an expensive, protracted, regulatory challenge — much tougher to do than it was in Grand Pappy's day. But a tank that has been in the ground for 30 years? Easy. Fill it up and roll.

Which means many of these petroleum distributors are sitting on sites with contaminated soil, marked by years of spills, and often surrounded by inadequate spill containment. No one wants to buy a petroleum distributor because of the liability threat. And because they are hard to sell, they tend to stay in the family for generations. They even tend to bear the family name.

I found myself in the lobbies of these companies, waiting patiently for my appointments with the owners. And I found the owners to be wonderful, down-to-earth people. The problem is that they moved half a million worth of product in the morning, and they planned to move another half-million gallons in the afternoon, and they were wary of that guy in the lobby who wanted to sell them 7,500 gallons of bio*what*?

They tended to pat me on the head, wish me luck, and send me on my merry way. "Go away, little boy," was understood.

Which was a problem for me.

Biodiesel tends to be distributed as a blend with petroleum. It finds its way into the world as "B20," which means 80% petroleum and 20% biodiesel. Or "B5," or "B2."

There I was with 100% biodiesel. I needed petroleum marketers to get my product into the world, and they weren't interested in my piddly volumes. But without a petroleum platform, I had no way to go to market. So I lined up a tanker truck and driver, and we got trained on how to buy petroleum from the rack, and the next thing I knew we were buying tanker loads of petroleum diesel, bringing them to our biodiesel plant, giving them a squirt of biodiesel, and sending them off to market.

Chris objected to the word "squirt." He was killing himself moving big liquids around, but the reality was that we would buy 6,000 gallons of petroleum, add 1,500 gallons of our precious biodiesel, and send it off into the world as "B20."

And in doing so we found we could easily beat the North Carolina State Contract price for B20. At the time, most of the biodiesel flowing into North Carolina came from Iowa — sort of the Walmart of biodiesel. And it costs twenty-six cents a gallon to move a gallon of biodiesel from Iowa to North Carolina by rail. Not a bad price advantage to wake up with, in a world that is traded to the tenth of a penny.

And so we started shipping. We picked up the Town of Cary. And the Town of Carrboro. And Chapel Hill. We picked up the Triangle Transit Authority for the region's buses, and began to see our fuel flow into the Wolfline at North Carolina State University. In no time much of the B20 in the area started coming from our plant, and we were delighted to watch our terminal fill up with biodiesel and sail out the door atop its petroleum counterpart. It turns out no one gets fired for paying less than the price stipulated on the State Contract.

There was one problem, however. And that was cash. When you buy petroleum at the rack, you pay cash. Everyone does. And you pay your share of state and federal taxes, which in North Carolina at the time amounted to around fifty-four cents a gallon.

Delivering a single load required a lot of cash — most of which was spent on petroleum, which was not our high-margin product. And since virtually all of our customers were government agencies, they were not required to pay taxes. Which meant we had to claw our prepaid taxes back from both the State of North Carolina, and the IRS. Doing that is fun and easy, but it took time. Lots of time before we would see our cash returned to us.

Plus, most of our fuel was delivered on terms. Bills are paid very quickly in the petroleum industry. Invoices turn in a matter of days — not weeks or months like some other industries. What all this boils down to is that shipping petroleum is a vastly cash-intensive business. My brother Mark was in charge of our financial engineering at the time, and he figured we would need three quarters of a million dollars a month of revolving cash in order to sustain our petroleum play.

And we didn't have it.

One of the outcroppings of this strategy was that we accidentally took 100% of the business away from the petroleum distributors. For us, shipping a 7500-gallon tanker load required 1500 gallons of our product. For the distributor who used to have the Chapel Hill account, it meant losing the entire business.

Which made our phones ring.

Next thing I knew my calendar was filled with petroleum distributors, many of who had lost business to us, who were curious to find ways in which we could work together. Many came to the plant for a tour, where they were greeted by me — that same little guy who once sat in their lobbies. The same fellow for which they previously had no use.

In no time our sales problem was fixed. Our million gallon per year biodiesel plant was happily included in the system that delivers four million gallons of petroleum diesel each day to those needing motive power in North Carolina.

Piedmont Biofuels exited the petroleum business immediately. The strategy introduced us to the world, but we learned that it is best to leave the petroleum business to those with the vast capital reserves, and the rolling stock, and the tankage. We were better off just making our cleaner burning renewable fuel.

By now we are well-known throughout the petroleum industry in our region, and we enjoy long and deep relationships with those petroleum distributors who traffic in biodiesel.

Something that perpetually amazes me is the extreme cooperation that exists in the industry in general. The public pumps its fuel under the misguided notion that Exxon is different from Shell, and that one brand is different from another. The reality is that it is simply about moving liquids around and has much less to do with product than it does with logistics. In a business that is as mature as petroleum, the product flows through many hands before reaching the consumer, and the profit margin left behind for each handler is so low that it becomes all about who has which truck where and when.

It is nothing for one distributor to lose a customer to another in the name of fetching a penny a gallon. Customers are not under contract, and are accustomed to leaving their suppliers for a tenth of a penny. Quotations go out to four decimal places and are good for the afternoon. Without bitterness, anger, or emotion, whole loads are lost and gained as a matter of course. Everyone is clear on one another's cost structure, and everyone is clear on who will make money on the transaction, and many of the transactions are completed harmoniously.

In North Carolina the public believes the business is character-ized by cutthroat competition, but it is not. Every time there is a hurricane, which pinches our vulnerable fuel supplies, our bone-headed Attorney General makes a speech about how he is going to look into price gouging.

The reality is that no one makes any money selling petroleum products "on the street." Selling gas is a way to get consumers to stop in. The money is made on potato chips, lottery tickets, and cigarettes. Think for a moment about the newly automated dispensers that offer television, credit card processing, and fuel at the same time. They have one over-arching message: stop inside.

Because one station posts a sign that reads 2.59.9, and the one across the street reads 2.58, the public believes that it is lock stock competition. Which it is not. Chances are good the same petroleum distributor owns each station, and the main objective of each is to sell more chocolate bars and coffee.

The money to be made in the oil business is not with the poor schmuck selling gasoline. And it is not with the third generation distributor who is deploying vast assets for thin margins. For a time I believed the vast profits must lie with those who pull oil out of the ground, but it turns out that can also be a marginal undertaking. Most of America's crude oil supplies today come from "stripper" wells, most of which are family owned, down on the ranch in Texas, Louisiana, and Oklahoma. Those are the lone pumping rigs in the middle of the field of cows or sagebrush, that are slowly going up and down like one of those glass birds with a belly full of water that is pretending to drink from a glass.

Many of these wells require something like sixty dollars of cost to produce a single barrel of oil, and many produce as little as ten barrels a day. So when you are driving down the road and hear that oil hit a record $61.00 a barrel, keep in mind that some fellow in Oklahoma could be fetching $10.00 that day.

The oil business is like any other. Everyone who is in it assumes there is more money to be made somewhere else. The producers envy the refiners, the refiners envy the pipelines, the pipelines envy the distributors, the distributors envy the gas station operators, and on it goes. The driving public, and the Attorney General, tend to be oblivious to the entire industry.

Surely fortunes have been made. And lost. People gamble. People win. People lose.

The notion that Piedmont Biofuels is any different from any other business undertaking is incorrect. We decided to become a processor. We developed an expertise in making fuel. Our petroleum equivalent would be the "refiner," and that is where we placed our bet.

As the industry matures, it turns out that making biodiesel is an extremely marginal activity. We spend our days wishing we were producers of feedstock. We wish we could create poultry fat, or crush seeds into oil, or be anywhere other than at the mercy of those who control the resource upon which we depend. But those who control our feedstocks envy our position, to make fuel. And those who are distributing the fuel have a prurient interest in our business as well, since they, too, are living on razor-thin margins.

We put our money on biodiesel. We were convinced it would either "win, place, or show." It's been a long race, and so far we have yet to scrape winnings off the table. We haven't given up, but the word to those who envy the producers of biodiesel is "Pick another horse."

Fortunately for Piedmont we don't just make biodiesel. On the winding road to our eco-industrial park, we spawned a number of internal and related businesses that allowed us to hedge our bets.

Accidental Diversification

I N JANUARY 2005, I shoved the security gate open and walked onto a three and half-acre campus with four buildings spanning roughly twenty thousand square feet. We had just acquired an empty industrial site.

It was creepy. Poison ivy climbed the walls, possums, groundhogs, and raccoons roamed freely about. The buildings creaked and groaned in the wind and with the slightest change of temperature.

The place was built in 1986 by a group of folks who wanted to invent a superior aluminum for use in fighter jets. They managed to get big water, and big sewer, and big electricity pulled out to the middle of nowhere, but as far as I can tell they never figured out "big jobs."

It closed in 1996, shortly after the Soviet Union folded in the Cold War. Their better aluminum was a victim of the peace dividend.

And the park sat empty for another ten years. The buildings were strange. Two-foot thick concrete blast walls and hinged roofs that were designed to let explosions "out." It was a white elephant on the edge of town — too complicated to even bulldoze.

We thought we could put our entire biodiesel operation in the second building, which is four stories tall and came complete with

The Plant began as a creepy, abandoned place.

a three story mezzanine that was already painted green and yellow — the colors of Piedmont Biofuels.

We were young. And naïve. I literally showed up in coveralls ready to fire up my acetylene torch to cut out some equipment to make room for our biodiesel plant. I thought the first job that lay before us was to convert the abandoned industrial scrap into cash. We had electric transformers, and thousand-dollar breakers, and hydraulic presses for as far as the eye could see.

Yet when I ventured into that market I was startled to learn that such equipment was everywhere. In order to sell the remnants of an industrial plant, someone needs to be investing in industrial gear. And in North Carolina, in 2005, it appeared as if we were the only enterprise in the region that was actually building a "factory."

Combine that with the fact that there were and are abandoned mills and industries across our state — many with transformers and breakers and hydraulic presses collecting dust.

I learned early on that if I was going to convert stuff into cash, the market would be China, the competition would be fierce, and

With plantings and art and businesses we brought the Plant campus to life.

selling off industrial gear would be a new career entirely. Rather than embark on a new career, we set about selling things off for scrap metal and went to work on designing and building our biodiesel plant.

Once I figured out how to turn the electricity on, I went to work on outfitting the original Control Room as our office space. I thought it would be a suitable place to make camp while we built. And it was horrific. Leif, me, and Evan set up on tables and desks side by side with no daylight, no fresh air, with two land lines and three cell phones and a fax machine. When Rachel decided to join us, I took my torches and cut a circular hole in the control room wall and gutted what was once a wiring closet. It was just enough space to fit a desk and a bookshelf. We called it the "Hobbit Hollow" because of the shape of the cut in the wall.

From that awful little control room we designed and built and permitted North Carolina's first B100 terminal — the first place in the state to get 100% biodiesel that wasn't off a rail car.

Two months into the endeavor I published an entry in Energy Blog entitled "Office Downgrade":

Blog

I thought that our office at Industrial was modest. I have a piece of plywood over a steel frame where I sit. But it is heated, and it has lights. We have a photocopier. And although it is close quarters, it works for now.

Today I came in to meet a team of electricians. The goal is to strip unwanted power that hangs in conduit from our proposed laboratory and proposed office space. Last week I had a chance to work with Tuesday again. We spent many years in the art business together, and we tapped her for some torch work at the plant. She cut out some enormous argon pipes to clear space for us. By shedding the pipes, and losing the electrical wires, we should be able to transform what was once an equipment room into a glorious office/lab/reception area.

Today I had visions of getting the electricians started, and retreating to a quiet Leif- and Evan- free office to work on *Biodiesel Power*.

I was going to be upstairs in the quiet office collecting my thoughts, and the electricians were going to be tracing circuits back to the distribution panels and eliminating them entirely.

Except to do that we killed power to the whole building.

Which means I am now on a pair of sawhorses, on the lawn outside of building #3. I fished a scrap of wood out of the pile for a desktop, and have run a hundred-foot extension cord out to my notebook.

It's supposed to get up to 55 today, slight breeze, and it's not bad here in the sun. I can occasionally hear the electricians grunt and holler from across the way.

Our meeting with the Fire Marshal went exceedingly well. Leif and I both have plenty of work ahead of us to meet his expectations, but it can all be achieved, and yesterday we were stoked about our prospects in general...

While Piedmont was innocently building a biodiesel plant in Building 2, Tami and Matt Schlegel and I were renovating Building 1. We didn't need it for anything. It had a nice loading dock, and a machine shop, and some office space. Tami rented it out to Eastern Carolina Organics, which put in a giant drive-in cooler and set up a distribution operation for getting produce to fancy restaurants and grocery stores throughout the region.

Tami and Matt worked with local mosaic artist Janice Reeves and Diane Swan, our celebrity cabinetmaker, and they transformed what was once a machine shop into a remarkable kitchen and break room. They stained the concrete floor, put in a clerestory window for day lighting, and a giant arched window. We have Alicia Ravetto to thank for our day lighting strategy. I bought Tami a plant-wall biofilter, for her birthday, and we had it built into the wall. It is basically an indoor air-cleaning device with a continuous flow of water. It anchored the room in a remarkable way.

I think everyone on project would agree that the kitchen was over the top. Custom concrete counter tops with embedded shards of stained glass, locally grown maple "worm eaten" cabinet wood, with artful homemade light fixtures, it became a powerful space — a complete counterbalance to our nasty office in the control room.

We had no idea what we were doing. In the creation of the kitchen we accidentally created a magnetic space that set the tone for the project. Suddenly people wanted to use it for board meetings. We outfitted it with chairs and tables and started accommodating groups. Some rented, some donated, many were free, and while the kitchen never became a "revenue stream," it meant the place filled up with groups from the Haw River

Assembly to the Chatham Soccer League — and everything in between.

Having the coolest meeting space in three counties made the biodiesel plant a destination. Which gave it buzz, and traffic, and filled our parking lot up with interesting and interested people.

In the beginning the buildings were surrounded by turf. I hate turf. Unless it gets used. I can't see the point of mowing something that no one sets foot on. Tuesday put together a pair of soccer goals such that one patch of turf could be a soccer field.

That made us a destination for soccer. In Small is Possible I wrote, "The plant is routinely a venue for parties. Children swarm to its midst with scooters and skateboards and inline skates, and all manner of wheeled devices. A whole generation will lose their training wheels at Piedmont Biofuels. That is either a reflection of our craving for community, or of the fact that we have a strip of safe pavement."

As the biodiesel plant progressed we were slammed to a halt by water pressure. We knew that we would have to install a sprinkler system for our high hazard work, but were caught off guard by the fact that we did not have enough water pressure to operate a sprinkler system.

After all, our abandoned industrial park was at the end of the water line on the edge of town. We only had enough water pressure to sprinkle two small rooms. Increasing pressure meant erecting a water tower. Which was a $350,000 surprise. By the time we encountered this problem, our money supply was running low and we had no way to pull it off.

So we wedged our reactors, and our high-hazard work into two small rooms in Building 3, and we built an underground pipeline that crossed the street. Whew. Good thing we had an extra building. Suddenly biodiesel would require both Building 2 and Building 3.

Upon doing so we hit another formidable snag. Building 3 was located very close to our property line. In order to pull off our plan, we would have needed to locate our tank farm, which included ten thousand gallons of methanol storage, right next to the adjoining property. We were hemmed in.

So we bought the surrounding property. That moved us from three and half acres up to a fourteen-acre campus. After closing, we ripped down a large section of fence, and built our tank farm.

As part of our cash recycling efforts, we sold Building 4 to Jacques and Wendy. They had a brisk trade in fabrics and imported art and antiques and Building 4 became their warehouse.

On one end of the campus we were giving it our all building a biodiesel plant. On the other end various businesses were popping up. Screech moved his hydroponics lettuce operation in. Piedmont Biofarm started farming the vacant lots that surrounded our buildings. Tracy Kondracki moved her "Green Bean Accounting" business into an empty office in Building 1. And the Abundance Foundation, which is driven by my wife Tami snatched up another empty office.

A stage in the lawn brought on rock concerts and festivals, and provided a venue for politicians to speechify about our low carbon future. Eventually Piedmont finished its office space, complete with a gorgeous second story porch, and moved into the new Control Room, where most of us still work today.

We found a room in Building 3 that could be converted to office space, and before the paint was dry it was rented to Cecellia as an office for her work with the North Carolina Wildlife Commission.

We came for the biodiesel. Baskets and produce and bookkeeping and lettuce were ancillary. Piedmont Biofuels accidentally became the anchor tenant of what would emerge as an eco-industrial park. What we failed to understand at the time, as we were bringing our chemical plant to life, was that we were imitating nature, and accidentally diversifying. As Piedmont Biofuels lumbered along, trying to find its way into the world of a cleaner burning renewable fuel, an eco-industrial park sprung up around it. Before we knew it there were seven unique businesses inside the fence.

Farmers were coming to drop off their wares. Some filled up with fuel in the yard.

Allen came along wanting some biodiesel as a feedstock for his bio-pesticide business. We had an empty floor on our mezzanine, so we designed and built a precision blending operation for him. That went well, and he eventually took over Building 4. On one side of the street we work hard to avoid emulsions. We then sell product to Eco Blend so that it can be emulsified. One side of the street hates free fatty acids. The other side of the street sells them for a living.

I should note that as the real estate all around us was filling up with tenants, and projects that were largely focused on sustainability, we were mostly oblivious. At the time we did not see ourselves as an escort into the low carbon future. We were merely building a biodiesel plant. Welding every weld and fitting every pipe ourselves.

Piedmont Biofuels suffers from an acute case of "Do It Yourself Syndrome," and because we had designed and built a handful of biodiesel projects, we found ourselves squarely in the design-build business for other people. Years ago we did a complete biodiesel plant on a trailer. Which led to a second version that became our Clean Technology Demonstration rig, which we drag around to various venues to demonstrate biodiesel production.

The North Carolina Zoological Park liked the notion of a biodiesel plant on a trailer so they hired us to build one for them. UNC Pembroke liked the notion too, so they bought one. As did Clemson University, and Hill Town Biodiesel Cooperative, as did Montana State University. By the time a principal at Washington High School decided to write a grant to build a biodiesel plant on a school bus, we had shipped a bunch of mobile units.

When the financial crash hit in the fall of 2008, our design-build group was staring at a year's worth of work, and delivering projects profitably. As the recession deepened, the work grew. Small-scale biodiesel, based on feedstock anomalies flourished, as the giant biodiesel plants — and the industry itself — began to falter.

We found ourselves offering engineering assistance to seed crushing facilities, and spending almost as much time making 3D models of how to move liquids around as we spent making biodiesel.

At the same time we entered the research and development business. Greg and David had invested a massive amount of time and energy in the development of a cavitational reactor for biodiesel production, which they were positioning for small scale plants, and Greg took his enthusiasm for the learning edge and hired on to a research project involving the creation of heterogeneous catalyst.

At the time Rachel was our quality manager. She shepherded us through the BQ-9000 accreditation process, which is a quality standard awarded by the National Biodiesel Board. We were the smallest biodiesel plant in the land to make the grade. Rachel joined Greg in his quest for science projects and we found ourselves building a second lab and entering the world of contract research and analytics.

In the spring of 2007, with some assistance from the Biofuels Center of North Carolina, we embarked on the creation of our second chemical plant, which we referred to as our "bio-refinery." In the course of creating biodiesel, a cocktail of co-products is created that largely has no market at all. Our bio-refinery was designed to sort that cocktail into its component parts, such that it could be turned into cash.

We turned on the bio-refinery in the fall of 2008, but we could not get it working properly until the summer of 2009. Once again we were a year late.

But by the fall of 2009, when the biodiesel industry had all but collapsed, our bio-refinery was spinning like a top, and we were able to bring in co-products from other biodiesel plants — those which were mostly closed, or idle, or waiting for the economy to turn. At the time we could land co-product feedstock for about a penny a pound, and after sorting it out in the bio-refinery, we were fetching thirteen cents a pound. Refining, it seemed, was a profitable undertaking.

Another important thing that occurred in the spring of 2009 was that the Board of Directors of the Piedmont Biofuels Coop elected to "become one" with Piedmont Biofuels Industrial. The Coop was a grassroots effort that was operating out of a double wide, collecting used vegetable oil from area restaurants, and spinning it into fuel for its members.

It was losing money at an amazing rate, and had run afoul of its landlord, its creditors, its neighbors, the local fire marshal, and was about to face the EPA in a showdown it had no hope of winning. Rather than letting a beloved institution fail, the Board decided to "land it in the Hudson," by merging it with Industrial.

When the Coop and Industrial became one, we ended up with a soap maker, who was happily making soap out of crude biodiesel glycerin. And we ended up with a rainwater collection business that was largely concerned with marrying the ubiquitous containers of chemical handling to homeowners attempting to combat our increasing drought conditions.

By the fall of 2009 we had been making biodiesel for seven years. We had used almost every feedstock imaginable, except human fat, and despite our labors, we had never made any money producing fuel. I'm guessing we had lost money on every gallon ever produced, and we had produced well over a million gallons of fuel.

The industry was on the ropes and Piedmont was no exception. In the cold grey days of October I was astonished to see that our biodiesel production had hit an all time low — about 2700 gallons in a month, from an asset capable of making 4000 gallons in a day. We were down more than 90% from the same period a year earlier.

Yet our campus was expanding. Dan was leading volunteers in the construction of a new pole barn for Piedmont Biofarm, which was profitable on its own head of steam, and building a new greenhouse. Screech was undertaking a bold expansion, moving his operation from a lone greenhouse inside the fence to five more up on the hill.

I was building a seed crushing facility in the hallway of Building 3, to ready us for both a workshop, and a load of sunflower seeds that had been grown in wastewater by the City of Raleigh.

A new era of education and outreach had begun. Used cooking oil collection was in full swing, and Rachel tasked her sister Andrea with the creation of a new tradeshow booth.

One of the panels on the new booth was to be "Products from the Plant," and Rachel and I went to work assembling photographs and verbiage.

Starting at the same gate I once shoved open as I walked into an abandoned industrial compound 4 years earlier, the list went something like this: Honey from Rick and his bees, organic produce from Eastern Carolina Organics, bookkeeping services from Tracy at Green Bean, festivals and events from the Abundance Foundation, biodiesel, rainwater delivery systems, vermiculture bins, boiler fuel, glycerin, design-build services and research from Piedmont Biofuels, produce and worm castings from Piedmont Biofarm, bio-herbicides and bio-pesticides from Eco-Blend, soaps from Deniece, and hydroponics lettuce from Screech.

Were we only making biodiesel, we would be bankrupt, like so many others. Instead we had accidentally diversified to the point of survival.

At the time I wrote about it in a column for the *Chapel Hill News* — which they titled "How Industry Evolves":

blog

In North Carolina, we tend to put our industrial sites in the southeast corner of every county. That's largely so that when our industries dump their pollution in our rivers, it becomes the problem of the county next door.

That way Alamance can have the effluent of its dye houses flow immediately into Chatham County, and Chatham County can have the effluent of its resin makers, and the heat from the Cape Fear coal fired power facility, flow readily into Harnett County, which put its denim plants in the southeast corner, and so on to the sea.

Historically "county government" has been much more powerful in the south than in other parts of the world. We are accustomed to our county sheriffs, and attorneys, and county managers wielding serious power.

I am presently immersed in the writing of my next book, tentatively entitled "Industrial Evolution." The other day over lunch Rachel and I were marveling over Piedmont Biofuels, accidental creation of a full-scale eco-industrial park in Pittsboro.

"It probably should have been in Moncure," she said.

That's where we both live. It's the southeast corner of Chatham County — where all the industry is.

Moncure is where we have rail access. That's a treasure for our economic development folks, since not every county has it. And Moncure is where we have cooling towers. And smokestacks. A few years ago Moncure was home to the highest emitter of formaldehyde in the land.

✿ ✿ ✿

Our project is "in town." And I suppose the reason we are in town is because we started with an abandoned industrial park. We were so focused on limiting the embodied energy of our project, that we couldn't see the point in breaking ground on a green field. Our job is to help escort North Carolina into a low carbon future, which is why we snagged a campus of abandoned buildings, rather than breaking ground on the rail spur.

Rail is about being "big." We want to make a go of it staying "small."

Today 75% of the biodiesel industry in America is boarded up. We still haven't figured out how to turn $3.00 oil into a $2.00 fuel. Piedmont is still chugging away.

For the past five years Rachel and I have driven past "For Rent" signs on our way to work. When the "Great Recession" hit we noticed an increase in abandoned buildings with signs in the yard. And yet there is a backlog of people who are trying to get space inside our fence.

Where we work, the co-products of one business are the feedstock of another, and the waste of one business becomes the heat source for the greenhouse on the hill.

In an economy that has allegedly ground to a halt, we are pulling building permits, and hiring builders. It appears the Abundance Foundation is about to move into the first "actually green" office building in Chatham County. And it's tucked into the back yard of a chemical plant — nestled up against the sustainable farm that surrounds us.

We offer free tours of the plant every Sunday afternoon at 1:00 —as we have always done — and we have noticed a newfound interest in sustainability. What was once "all biodiesel all the time" has shifted ever so slightly into an interest in our rainwater delivery systems, and our worm castings, and our vermiculture digesters, and the banana trees that grace our campus.

This year we are not going to have to argue about climate change. We will simply show our guests a locally grown banana. At long last our banana trees in the yard are bearing edible fruit.

When you go down to the industrial plants in Moncure, you tend to be stopped by a security guard. Free tours are hard to come by.

And while both Rachel and I live down that way, I think we are glad to go to work in town…

In the early eighties I was fortunate enough to hire on to my brother Jim's computer distribution business. I started out

Lyle was delighted with his first edible banana harvest.

hanging drywall in his office, became a technical writer for his fledgling custom engineering group, moved into order processing when the administrative anchor of the business, Suzanne, quit. From there I launched a career in sales. We were lucky. Jim started selling computers out of the trunk of his car before Microsoft was invented. When IBM entered the industry we successfully retooled our business and our business exploded like the industry itself.

Microsoft's founder, Bill Gates went on to become the wealthiest man on earth and a popular computer evangelist. I met him once, on the show floor of the first ever "Windows World" in Atlanta where he rode the escalator like all the rest of us. And he was gracious, thanking people for coming to his show.

But I always thought Bill Gates was confused. He was always preaching "convergence" in which all of our technologies would arrive at the same point, and do everything for us. That struck me as being the opposite of how things happen in nature. In nature, species divide, they don't converge. I believe the same logic holds true for business. Businesses naturally diverge.

The world that Bill Gates described had us balancing our checkbooks, and getting our entertainment, and reading our books on one splendid device that would allow all of our needs to "converge." Yet it seems to me I have multiple devices piling up. My boys have a Wii console for playing one type of computer game and are saving up for an Xbox to allow them a wider range of game choices. I have a notebook computer where I tend to do different work than I do with our desktop model, and apparently I am in need of a separate electronic device with which I can download the books I want to read. While it is true that my cell phone has way more computing firepower than I can possibly understand, it's not where I play games or do my banking.

I think "divergence" is what business does. When my brother Jim's custom engineering business was floundering, he spun it out as a stand-alone company, where it found a niche and prospered.

That is certainly what Piedmont has done.

Another juncture where we depart from mainstream corporate America is when it comes to sharing information. We are the originators of "Open Biodiesel," which borrowed heavily from the software industry.

In the software world there is a radical notion called "open source," where the source code is often free to its users. In the parlance of the open source world, it is "free as in speech, not free as in beer."

At the heart of the open source software proposition is the notion of a "community" of developers who work together to improve the product such that new features and functions can evolve rapidly. "Release early, and release often" is a common mantra from the world of open source.

The idea is that a small company with a community of contributors can have a larger development reach than it can afford, thereby permitting it to compete with giant "proprietary" competitors with large bankrolls.

In *Small is Possible*, I discussed how the principles of open source software development spilled over into community scale biodiesel. This caught the attention of Michael Tiemann, one of the founders of the open source movement.

Michael invited me out to his company, Red Hat, to speak to a lunchtime crowd as part of their "Lunch and Learn" speaker series. That began a friendship that has spanned a bunch of readings, and speaking events, and panel discussions in the public eye that are not half as interesting as the lunches and breakfasts we have had along the way.

At one point he introduced us to Tim O'Reilly's venture capital firm. Rachel and Leif and I found ourselves in a San Francisco board room discussing our little biodiesel project with some extremely interested, well heeled, and powerful members of the open source community.

When Red Hat launched opensource.com they invited me to contribute something on how open source principles can transcend the software industry. Here is the column I wrote called "Open Biodiesel":

Blog

_____

I've had a number of career changes. I went from poetry to technology to metal sculpture to the Internet to biodiesel. And I must admit that although I have brushed against "open source" a number of times, I have had a hard time getting my head around it.

Once I was working the show floor of USENIX in San Antonio, in 1998, the year Free BSD was released. It created quite a buzz. But I wasn't sure what to do with such a thing.

I later ended up as the CEO of an Internet company. The "bubble" had burst, the company I was to run was pretty much bankrupt, and my job was to fix it. As part of the turn around I invested in OpenNMS, which is an open source network management company. At the time I still didn't know what "open source" meant.

OpenNMS was (and still is) run by Tarus Balog. He's a charismatic champion of the movement and I quickly fell under his spell.

Tarus told me to read *The Cathedral and the Bazaar,* which I did. Tarus took me to the Triangle Linux User Group. For a moment in time "open source" was my life.

I'm not really a "turn around" guy. My brother Mark used to joke about my work on the Internet, saying, "They wanted a 'turnaround artist' and all they got was an 'artist.'"

During my time with OpenNMS I was migrating toward biodiesel. Biodiesel is a cleaner burning renewable fuel that is made from fats, oils, and greases. I was making the stuff in my back yard, and signed up for the fledgling Bio-Fuels program at Central Carolina Community College.

I was busy scaling up biodiesel, and scaling down my life in the technology sector. Technology was making me narcoleptic. Biodiesel was lighting my fire. Tarus and OpenNMS went on to build an open source success story, while I abandoned them for a fifty-five gallon drum and a canoe paddle.

I jumped in with Leif and Rachel (my instructors at the college), and together we founded Piedmont Biofuels. We had some early successes making fuel and were immediately confronted with a critical decision: Should we tell the world what we had learned or should we keep it a secret in order to parlay our knowledge into cash?

We decided to take an "open" approach, and instead of applying for patents, and sealing our lips, we published our successes and failures on Energy Blog. Our work was free for the entire world to see.

At the time the biodiesel industry in America was in its infancy, and as such it was shrouded in proprietary secrets and great advances, and complicated licensing schemes.

Our work stood in stark contrast to an evolving industry, in which charlatans came and went, and "black box" solutions regularly emerged and disappeared. It was the Wild West for biodiesel and no one was sure what stories to believe.

Piedmont's notion of "open source biodiesel" immediately got traction in the grassroots biodiesel community and became the standard for how small projects should interact with one another. We had our flops. And we had our successes. And we published them all.

In no time we found ourselves with an active consulting business. Our rates went from being a member of our Coop ($50.00 per year) to $50.00 per hour to $100.00 an hour to $200.00 dollars an hour in order to slow things down a bit. I've often thought, "Tarus would be proud."

As public money started flowing into our project in the form of grant awards, we stuck to the knitting. We offered free tours, and free information to anyone. Interest in our project built rapidly. Part of our message to public funders was that we would tell anyone anything they wanted to know.

The fact that we were open source appealed to those with public money. I'm not sure any of us clearly knew what it meant, but funders wanted to know that if they bestowed grant money upon us, our stewardship of that money would benefit others. As a result we accidentally became a frequent recipient of both federal and state grants.

But our commitment to open had a broader benefit. The biodiesel industry has had a bruising ride since its inception. The public doesn't really understand biofuels, and the industry doesn't tend to be "open" in an effort to make itself clear.

When we were making fuel in the backyard we were quirky. For a moment there, when biofuels were going to save the world, we were sexy. We had a moment as rock stars. But when global commodity markets climbed to record highs in the summer of 2008, the whole food vs. fuel debate came to the fore and biofuels became evil. That's when our industry made the cover of *TIME* magazine as a sham. And that's when the United Nations accused those responsible for making biofuels of being guilty of "crimes against humanity."

We went from quirky to sexy to evil, and we continued to publish our stories along the way. As a result we had credibility that allowed us to survive where others died. As biofuels projects collapsed under the weight of "evil," we persevered on the strength of our transparency alone.

We have been "open" at every step along the way, and we feel that our openness has been critical to the success of our enterprise.

At Piedmont Biofuels we have a lot of "firsts." We have a number of breakthroughs under our belt. And we have shared both our "firsts" and our breakthroughs freely with the world along the way, and we have watched our industry rise and fall as it fumbles about with policy decisions that will determine the role of biodiesel in our energy mix.

By some measures it is fair to characterize community-scale biodiesel as an industry that is open. Surely we receive as many good ideas as we contribute. And there is no doubt that we have benefited greatly from the community of small-scale producers.

Just as the small open source software company can successfully compete with much larger proprietary rivals, our small biodiesel company looms larger than life because of its many contributions to industry knowledge.

Which might not matter in the least. We still haven't figured out how to eat fame. And we are still paying off the vast "tuition" we have paid as pioneers in the biodiesel industry. But we are resilient. And we are "open." And we wear both of those monikers with pride.

We came for the fuel, and after a few sharp detours, found ourselves intact because of all the divisions along the way. When fuel production was down, design-build was booming when design-build was soft, our research and analytics would sometimes carry the day. We've diverged. We've held on. We've innovated. And we feel that our accidental diversification is rather the way things occur in nature, and that it is a critical reason we are still alive.

Local Food Friday

ON ANY GIVEN FRIDAY a visitor to the plant who happened by at noon would hear the dinner bell ring and would be invited to stay for lunch.

Lunch would be prepared by a team of three to five volunteers who would have banded together throughout the week to put on an amazing spread for fifty to sixty enthusiastic eaters.

The food tends to come from across the street. Or sometimes from the other side of town. It has become an over-the-top study in excess, where giant platters of Eliza's sausage, or slabs of mahi-mahi caught by Jacques and his kids are passed about by the meat eaters, while exquisite dishes of homemade tempeh and seitan are relished by the vegans in our midst.

We chose Friday as the lunch day because it was the day after the Pittsboro farmers market, and we wanted to ensure that the volunteer teams could avail themselves of local food.

But hyper-localism soon kicked in, and people started labeling where each ingredient came from, leading to snide remarks like, "These are remarkable new potatoes, Matt, where did you get them?"

"Doug grew them. They came from 100 yards from the kitchen."

"Nice. What's with the far-away ketchup?"

Peer pressure, and sport, and conviviality have descended on "Local Food Friday," and it has become a durable institution on our project. Surely there are potlucks over at Oilseed Community, and on the bend in the Moncure Road, and there are a myriad of "family" dinners across project, where people persistently dine together without being "family" at all, but Local Food Friday is one place where almost all of us gather once a week.

Those who participate go through considerable effort to collect and prepare enough food for fifty, and then eat every Friday for free for eight or nine weeks after that. Teams form, people float from team to team based on food they procure, teams break up and reform, and it moves along.

Because there are humans involved, frictions arise. One challenge was the arrival of the "dumpster divers." Those enthusiastic eaters who rummage through the food waste of area grocery stores, and

Local eaters from across the project gather for Local Food Friday lunch.

provided their treasures to the rest of us. My first "dumpstered" dish was lamb that had been retrieved from behind a Trader Joes, and I remember marveling at how such an exquisite meal could have emerged from the largess of the machine.

Some of our eaters were squeamish about eating dumpstered food and insisted that it be labeled. Others felt that developing a dependency on a dumpster signaled an unsustainable relationship to the commodity food shed.

Since then, Moya has taken the whole notion up a notch by filling the company fridge with her "off spec" dairy program. She intentionally intercepts dairy products that are about to be thrown away and brings them onto project with a "use at your own risk" message. And they do get used.

There are other disputes, of course. There is the vegan camp that wants every ingredient labeled, and the carnivorous camp who wants to serve up monster racks of Emily's "happy pig" ribs, and would like to merely pound a sign in the grass outside the kitchen with a label that says, "vegan option."

There is also the problem of guests. Guys like me like to invite multiple people to Local Food Friday, such that I can knock out three meetings or obligations at a time. I'm guessing there is a bit of my brother Jim's influence here. He is a time management guru, and he would approve of how I can cover a lot of ground with a lot of people in the least amount of time. But serving guests puts a strain on the budget, and so a "donations" fund has emerged in which guests throw some money into the pot and the pot is spent on staples like cooking oil and honey and molasses.

People have dropped out because it is too loud, or because preparing a sit down meal for fifty is overwhelming, but at its core Local Food Friday is a solid fixture that functions well.

What is less known about this institution is that it had its roots in the company lunch room of twenty years ago where a number of us would gather in our coats and our ties with our brown-bag fare.

I would turn to Steve and say, "You know, I could make you lunch everyday next week if you would reciprocate the week after that."

Steve would reflect on the offer, and agree, and I would go out and shop for the two of us. That was an era before I understood my relationship to energy, or had ever contemplated local food. I recall those lunches as being well stocked with potato chips.

Steve and I would be happily sharing the lunch burden together and someone else at the table would enquire as to what we were doing, and I would explain that it was the "Communist Lunch Plan," in which food was shared between us, and I would invite them to join. And they would. And one of us would find ourselves delivering five lunches for three, and taking weeks off. And so on.

The Communist Lunch Plan would build, and then collapse under its own weight. For her week, Tami would go to Fresh Market and spend a fortune on exotic nuts and chocolates and deli meats with artisan bread. We would be appreciative of her efforts and enjoy her week, and the next week Skip would come in with bargain basement corned beef vacuum packed from the Sav-A-Lot, causing Tami to storm out, announcing that she would never participate in Communism again.

At which point the entire program would collapse, everyone involved would cite the reasons they preferred to dine exclusively on their own food, and we would all be back to our individual brown bag lunches.

Months would pass, and I would suggest to Steve that I would make his lunches for a week if he would agree to reciprocate. He would agree and Communism would rise again.

This pattern ensued for many years. I suppose it informed my thinking about the commons. Communism would rise and fall, the company grew and grew and it was not unusual to have a half dozen communists sharing lunch together at a table with a half dozen skeptics, and a couple of avowed individualist eaters.

I sold that company to the employees, and the new owners of the firm were skeptical of the Communist Lunch Plan. But I suspect they saw some sort of morale value in bringing people together for a common meal, so they instituted "Grill Thursday," in which one group of people would take turns grilling for the others.

Grill Thursday worked for a while. It became an eclectic mix of people in an office building that housed a variety of firms. At the time I was entering into biodiesel, and I entered a "team" that would cook for everyone on our appointed Thursday. We were migrating deep into low energy food production and organics that was at odds with the palette of some. One eater claimed to be on doctor's orders not to eat organic. It was bizarre. And the same thing that would repeatedly break the Communist Lunch Plan would happen to Grill Thursday. Tarus would bring in his propane tank and stand to deep fry a turkey when it was his week, and would quit the program all together when the next week he was served generic hot dogs on commodity buns.

Michael Pollan, author of *The Omnivore's Dilemma*, makes some astute observations about food and cooking. He suggests that Americans spend so much time watching cooking shows that they have no time to cook. He cites Richard Wrangham's book, *Catching Fire*, when he suggests that cooking has been central to human evolution.

From an academic perspective the argument goes like this: because humans discovered how to cook, they could eat a wider range of foods, and because of that required less in the way of stomach, allowing for more in the way of brain. Not so for the cow. Adapted only to eat grass, it requires three guts to extract the food energy it needs. Yet nowadays the process appears to be working in reverse. Our food supply has become so over- processed and prepared, so cut with chemicals and non-food fillers that we are requiring more in the way of the gut. I'm not sure of the technical term for it. Human beings have started evolving in reverse?

I run a lot of Pollan's work through the filter of Tami's family. Her grandmother Ruby worked like a dog all her life. She canned, and cooked, and preserved the food her husband grew on the farm, at the same time holding down a job at a local department store in Raleigh. Unlike the cooking-show viewer of today, who presumably gets a lot of time on the couch, Ruby spent most of her time working to feed the family.

Ruby's daughter Anne got a pass on the cooking grind. By the time she came along food was pre-prepared for her. It was cheap, and abundant, so she didn't have the need to invest in cooking. Which is why, when I met her daughter Tami, Tami simply couldn't cook. Her inability to cook, in fact, was legendary amongst her friends.

When we moved in together, I did all the cooking. Our only appliance at the time was a woodstove, which meant I subsequently started off almost every meal with bacon. A hot frying pan, pre-oiled with bacon grease was always a good start point. And from there, Tami not only learned to cook, but went on to become an excellent chef. Nowadays most people, who are intimate with the two of us, put Tami at the head of cooking for our household — which is at least true for those who have had her biscuits.

What I find intriguing is the yearning on our project to go back to the Ruby days. People have become so obsessed with meeting their own food needs that they belong to multiple CSAs, and run expansive gardens, and are taking up deer hunting, and figuring out ways to process foods for storage. We are returning to Ruby's almost-lost arts in the name of increased nutrition, or in the name of food security, or in the name of increased self-reliance.

The weakness of Grill Thursday was the disparate relationships to food within the group. There were those of the "convenience generation" offering up fare to those of the local/organic crowd. Some locavores were serving up food to folks who cared less about the ingredients than about the performance of the recipe. Perhaps, as a collection of eaters, it was too diverse. It didn't work very well. The final collapse of Grill Thursday was a great relief to all involved. People who care deeply about what they eat should not attempt to dine with those who could not care less.

The lessons learned from Grill Thursday formed a valuable building block in the creation of Local Food Friday. I should note that Local Food Friday often collides with our First Friday Tours, for which I am frequently the tour guide. One memorable collision was between a group of retirees from Clayton, North

Local Food Food Friday often spills out of the kitchen into the yard.

Carolina, and Jason and Haruka from Edible Earthscapes. We tend to think of Edible Earthscapes as part of our project, even though it is five miles from our eco-industrial park.

On this occasion Jason and Haruka were simply in the kitchen preparing stuffed peppers with rice because it "was their week." Their apprentice, Devon was also helping out. My tour group was early, and standing about in the kitchen, and the conversation came around to rice, which they are now growing at Edible Earthscapes. When I came in to pick up my charges, they were enthralled with Jason, and the notion that we could grow rice here. He was holding court, talking about water requirements and varieties and how he was on his way to Japan to pick up a rice-hulling machine.

Jason was used to it. Tourism is so engrained in our corporate culture that, he simply set down his paring knife and started explaining his rice project. I became interested too, but had to interrupt to pull the group away in order to start our tour on time.

And while this is a normal interaction for us, Local Food Friday is often jarring for the uninitiated. While we find it completely normal for a few farmers to be filling the kitchen with stuffed peppers for a forty person sit down lunch, and taking time out to discuss their rice experiment with visitors, our visitors often leave scratching their heads in wonder at what they have just encountered.

One of my regrets is that we did not design our kitchen with food service for fifty in mind. The space was constructed as a break room. The fact that it routinely bursts at the seams speaks to our urgent need for a commercial kitchen that will allow us to not only serve meals large enough for the whole project, but also allow us to move into legally canning, preserving, and selling the myriad varieties of food we have on our project.

Food is an interlocking piece in the evolution of our project. We have a large number of eaters who truly value the food produced, which leads to growers that are deeply appreciated for the work they do. Appreciation leads to meaningful work, and the consumption of that work leads to a deeper appreciation all around.

Our approach to food on project is to produce it year round. Our first greenhouse was a monstrous ninety-foot affair heated by wood. Since then Screech erected a thirty footer for hydroponics lettuce production. Then we added another thirty footer for Piedmont Biofarm, thinking it would be a good way to house our worm composting experiment. Then Screech doubled his

Matt Rudolf participates in preparing a lunch for dozens of guests.

operation. Then Piedmont Biofarm ordered another ninety-foot greenhouse, at which point Screech decided to put up four more thirty-foot greenhouses, and go into peppers, tomatoes, and cucumber production.

A large part of successful food marketing is season extension. If you are growing tomatoes, for instance, the trick is to have your product on the grocer's shelves before anyone else, in early spring, and to be out of the tomato business before everyone has them in abundance in their backyard gardens. Surely the master of this was Jim LeTendre, who routinely stunned the region with bountiful loads of "Sunny Slope" tomatoes.

Because season extension is key, a visitor to the plant will see row covers to offset sunlight at hot times of the year, and plastic to shield peppers from frost from time to time.

We eat seasonally, and we focus on year-round food. Fall brings a mushroom harvest from the woods and deer meat fills our freezers. It's not long before the bananas have been eaten and the peanuts have been devoured, but even in the dead of winter we are feasting on greens and sweet potatoes and we look forward to the February carrot harvest.

Our approach is not planned. It just is. And because we are surrounded by food production, food is not something we worry about whenever the conversation turns to complete societal collapse.

I have a dear friend who has taken the Mormon approach. He brings in big bins of red beans and flour and has a room in his basement dedicated to a year's supply of food. He claims it is hard to come by — difficult to buy rations in bulk — and he is pondering the formation of a new web-based company that would make it easier for people to stock up.

I wonder about the "store your own food approach," and if perhaps it is exactly the mentality that brought our world to the brink of collapse in the first place. The notion of individual stores of food is about the polar opposite of our project. What we do is contribute what we can. Fence posts, or labor, or cash, or soil amendments to the folks who grow the food, and in exchange we find ourselves not only well fed, but also not in fear of food shortages.

As I was working on this manuscript, Elinor Ostrom was awarded the Nobel Prize for Economics, and when Michael Tiemann pointed out the "Ostrom-like" nature of our project, I paid attention.

I don't think of our project as "radical," but I think it would be safe to call Ostrom that. For many years she sat in the wilderness screaming about the wrong headedness of the Chicago School (supply side, trickle down, the Milton Friedman types), and after a career of publishing, teaching, researching, and hollering, she was awarded a Nobel Prize.

As far as I can tell, the crux of Ostrom's argument is that a committed group of grassroots enthusiasts can do a better job managing a collective resource than can individual ownership, or can government regulations. So if we are thought to be "Ostrom-like," I'm going to take that as a compliment and move on. And I think there is certainly a grain of truth to it as far as our food shed is concerned. What we grow tends to be determined by eaters, or farmers, or both, and the simple reality of it is that we have enough people who care about local food to make a market that is worthy of supplying.

To be fair, we are rural. And we have a vibrant food shed, consisting of various food enterprises, including Chatham Marketplace, our cooperative grocery store and Eastern Carolina Organics (ECO), our organic food distributor. One of the miraculous benefits of having ECO as a tenant neighbor is that they periodically end up with product they cannot sell.

One of their growers might consider their strawberries to be "fancy," only to find that according to ECO they are not, which means they cannot be sold the way they were intended. That occasionally orphans truckloads of food.

In the early days of the plant, ECO paid Dean to haul off their food waste to his commercial composting facility. Dean has been a good friend to our project, since he not only operates one of the larger commercial composting sites on the eastern seaboard, he also has a giant fleet of rolling stock that he lets us hire for field clearing and pond building and tank lifting and the like.

Apart from his vast machinery resources, Dean also has wisdom and experience, which I have tapped many times over the years, and for which I am grateful.

Dean is a savvy operator, and he attempts to make money on every transaction he encounters. Which means if you are ECO Organics and you hire him to collect your food waste, it gets expensive.

Fortunately for ECO the project has grown to the point that anytime they need a few pallets of organically grown strawberries to disappear, they simply send out an email.

It's fun to watch eaters converge at the doors of ECO's dock on days when they are looking for homes for a ton of potatoes (because they have grey splotches), or truckloads of collards because some deal went south.

Wherever there is a food industry, there is a tremendous amount of food waste, and by embedding ourselves in the midst of farms and food purveyors, we find ourselves awash with the stuff.

And I think that wastage, in and of itself, is an appropriate lens through which to look at the biodiesel part of our project.

5

Piedmont Biofuels Industrial

WHEN WE STARTED commercial production of biodiesel in 2006 the industry was predicated on a simple assumption: buy a pound of fat, make it into biodiesel and throw about twenty percent away. To our dismay, it proved impossible to make money doing that.

By now everyone knows what biodiesel is. It's that cleaner burning renewable fuel that is derived from fat. To make biodiesel we start with fat — any fat, from soybean oil to poultry fat to olive oil — whatever, we mix it with a catalyst and with methanol and presto, biodiesel is formed.

The big word for it is "transesterification," in which we are creating methyl esters. When we make biodiesel we create a nice runny fuel that can be burned directly in any diesel engine. No going under the hood. No mechanic required. The fat has been chemically modified to suit the engine, so we just drive away.

One of the co-products of the reaction is an annoying cocktail that is hard to deal with. It contains some left over methanol (which makes it flammable), and it contains some free fatty acids (which didn't convert into biodiesel during the reaction), and it contains some glycerin, which is a thick viscous substance that you wouldn't want anywhere near the combustion chamber of your diesel engine. Glycerin is an alcohol. So is methanol. So at its rudimentary best, making biodiesel is simply about swapping alcohols around.

Which is sort of how Piedmont Biofuels began. I exhausted that topic in my first book, *Biodiesel Power: The Passion, the People and the Politics of the Next Renewable Fuel*. It is sort of a chronicle of how we started brewing biodiesel in my backyard, how we went on to form what became the largest biodiesel cooperative in America, and it ends just as we are thinking about buying an abandoned industrial park on the edge of town.

In that book I describe the cocktail that comes off of the biodiesel reaction as worthless, and in hindsight I cannot believe how wrong that was. That was the industry thinking at the time. I wasn't the only one who was dead wrong.

A bunch of us left the Coop and built Piedmont Biofuels Industrial, which was to be a million gallon per year biodiesel plant. That worked. The plant was designed to receive full eighteen-wheelers of fat, spin it into fuel, and ship full eighteen-wheelers of biodiesel out the gate.

For a while there we shipped a full truckload every other day, and we put many gallons of biodiesel into the world. I believe our best month ever was one hundred and twenty thousand gallons. We were pleased with how the asset performed.

And during those go-go days, our operations were predicated on sheer waste. We shipped the lion's share of our glycerin cocktail off to compost. And we didn't make any money doing it. The composters loved us, but it was not a path to riches.

When it became clear to us that any profits we might see lay in that twenty percent waste stream, we went to work on building our second chemical plant. This one we called our bio-refinery.

I should point out that I misused the word refinery about five hundred times in *Biodiesel Power*. That's the word we used back then, despite the fact that it is a misnomer. When you make

Full tankers of biodiesel typically leave our terminal to be blended downstream with petroleum diesel.

biodiesel you are not "refining" anything. You are reacting stuff. It just wasn't in our vocabulary to say, "See you tonight at the reactionary..."

Yet when it came to sorting out the cocktail of waste, refining is actually the correct term. Just as a petroleum refiner puts crude oil into its process, and extracts a variety of products from a "stack" of products, we set out to do the same thing with our cocktail.

With a generous $250,000 loan from the Biofuels Center of North Carolina, and an additional $250,000 in private investment, we set out to build our bio-refinery.

First we would get the mixture hot, to transform the liquid methanol therein to a gas, then we would run the gas through a condenser, attached to a chiller, at which point it would turn back into a liquid again, allowing us to "recover," or get our methanol back.

We wanted our methanol to come back in good shape such that it could be used again, but ours ended up bringing too much water with it, giving us drums of wet methanol that we piled up in the yard.

Once we had the methanol out, we gave the remaining cocktail an acid wash in a glass-lined reactor where it would split into two phases: free fatty acids and glycerin. We would take the free fatty acids and sell them as animal feeds or for boiler fuels, leaving us with just glycerin.

Once we had the glycerin cleaned up we found we could readily sell it. It is shipped by the tanker load as a surfactant for applications like dust suppression, and as a "release agent" in the coal industry. The glycerin is pure carbon, and it is an alcohol, so it lowers the freezing point of a pile of coal when it is sprayed on. That keeps the handling of the coal easy.

There are lots of other industrial applications for industrial glycerin, and when our bio-refinery came online in the winter of 2009, we started shipping full loads — thereby turning some of our waste into cash.

Our bio-refinery takes a lot of heat to operate correctly, and we initially brought it online using electric heaters, which we rapidly attempted to replace with boilers. We figured out how to use the boilers to burn the free fatty acids that came out of our glycerin cocktail.

Like so many of our efforts, this was not a trivial undertaking. Boilers like a consistent stream of fuel at all times, and they monitor that consistency in part with an electric eye. The electric eyes of the boiler world are looking for a petroleum- colored flame — which we didn't have, since we were attempting to burn free fatty acids, not petroleum boiler fuel.

As a result our boiler kept shutting down. So we yanked the firebox out, spray painted it a different color to fake out the electric eye, and solved that problem. We then went on to replace incompatible pump seals, and pumps, and by the time we were finished, after six months of putzing with it, we were deriving heat for our bio-refinery from free fatty acids. The system worked so well that we added another, and once we got all of the pipes insulated we were able to shut off our electric heaters and power our bio-refinery on free fatty acids alone.

We currently run two half-million-BTU boilers, meaning we throw a million BTUs an hour at bio-refining operations, which is all the heat we need to sort out the cocktail. When we are running wide open, smoke from our smokestack is undetectable. The North Carolina Division of Air Quality has been out to see this system, and has given it a clean bill of health. And it helped us convert more of our cocktail into money.

At the time Uncle Sam was paying a $0.50/gallon "burn credit" to anyone who could convert biomass to process heat, and our custom system qualified nicely. Instead of paying $0.16 a gallon to tip free fatty acids at the commercial composter, we were claiming the credit, which was a nice reversal.

In the fall of 2009 we at last found a buyer for our wet methanol, and at long last we had markets for all of the co-products of biodiesel production.

With the bio-refinery operating we are now able to convert every ounce of feedstock into cash. Nowadays when we buy a pound of fat, we turn it all into money. When once we could make 100K gallons in a month, and no money, we can now turn a profit on a mere 10K gallons a month. Goodbye waste, hello profit.

By wringing the waste out of our manufacturing process we can make a profit on every gallon of fuel, even when we are producing less gallons at our facility.

That fixation on converting our waste streams into money came about a year late. By the time we had our bio-refinery spinning like a top, most of the biodiesel industry was shutting down.

I think Piedmont tends to be a year late in general. Probably because we do everything ourselves.

By the fall of 2009 the cost of feedstock was so high that no one could afford to turn it into fuel. On paper, our bio-refining operations were a dream. We could take in the co-product of neighboring biodiesel plants for free, or for a penny a pound transportation charge, we could sort out the cocktail into its component parts, and we could convert it into valuable cash. Finally, refining made sense. Just as the industry was boarding up its plants, and just as our own production fell off the charts.

With the plant performing beautifully, we found our production limited to those feedstocks we could collect. Moya and Russell were out there killing themselves signing up restaurant accounts and dropping off barrels to gather used cooking oil at food service establishments throughout the region, but our biodiesel production was down to about three thousand gallons a month.

Our work on converting waste into money did show promise with other customers however. Screech went ahead and installed a "district heating" system in his greenhouse compound up on the hill, and another greenhouse operator near Charlotte did the same. We found ourselves designing and building custom boiler systems, and then furnishing those systems with free fatty acids or straight vegetable oil as fuel.

And we were busy working on converting all other co-products into cash. When we make biodiesel we use water to wash out impurities, and we noticed that whenever we disposed of our wash water, we threw some biodiesel away each time.

Greg figured out that by giving our wash water an acid bath he could emulsify the biodiesel within and remove it from our wash water stream. His recovered biodiesel ended up with too high an acid number to be legally sold for onroad use, so once again, we burned it in our boilers.

Better to convert a gallon of waste into 50 cents than to pay to send it down the drain.

Yet another ubiquitous part of the chemical industry is what is referred to as a "tote." They are large plastic cubes inside aluminum frames that typically hold two to three hundred gallons of liquids. In the trade they are known as "one way totes" since no one will take them back. As such they end up everywhere. They are nigh on impossible to clean and they can be see piled up as an annoying waste stream wherever big liquids are frequently handled.

In order to start finding homes for totes, we started cutting them in half. Bob started using beat up, grease-encrusted half totes for his container gardens. He took a patch of unproductive dirt out behind Camille and his residence at Oilseed Community — which they called "Camelina," and stunned everyone with what a fecund and productive garden could be had. He started teaching "square foot gardening" down at Central Carolina Community College and suddenly a market for wasted totes was born.

We started cleaning them and using them in rainwater delivery systems, and they eventually found their way into our worm bin designs.

For us totes represent "money in the yard," and as such need to be converted from something that simply takes up space into money that can go to work on the project.

And so, by the fall of 2009 we were doing really well with waste stream processing. Sami Grover over at Treehugger wrote that the "folks at Piedmont are 'systems thinkers of the highest order.'" That felt good. We think he had it right.

But kind words didn't change our perilous cash situation, or solve our huge feedstock limitation problem, and in the fall of 2009 there were periods of extreme darkness when I feared we would need to shut the business down.

The reality is that up until November of 2009, Piedmont Biofuels was a sinkhole for cash. Our Coop never made money. On an occasional year we would show a modest profit, but that was only when we didn't service debt, didn't pay interest, didn't pay for little things like biodiesel reactors and ion exchange columns, and as long as we hid behind our Industrial operation to stay safe with the fire marshal.

Our Industrial story was dramatically different. We started with a bunch of money, and we burned through it like corn through a goose.

Generally there is a rule of thumb in the biodiesel industry of a dollar of capital cost per gallon per year. In other words, if you want to build a million gallon plant, have a million dollars handy.

We built our initial plant for $881,000, and the year it hit peak stride it made almost 1.3 million gallons of fuel. Which looks good on paper. The reality, however, was that we spent two years coming on line. We are proud of the fact that we fitted every pipe ourselves, and drew every bead on every weld, but we missed the first profitable window for biodiesel production in America. The year biodiesel manufacturing made money was 2005. That's the year the industry pumped out about a hundred million gallons of product. That's the year the IRS offered a $1.00 per gallon production credit, and the Commodity Credit Corporation offered a feedstock subsidy to biodiesel producers. That was the year to make fuel.

We were welding tanks in place and missed it entirely.

When our production came online in the fall of 2006, the feedstock subsidy had ended and soybean oil (our feedstock at the time) was becoming unaffordable as a biodiesel feedstock.

We were commissioning our shiny new chemical plant just as the global soy markets were moving soybean oil beyond our reach.

I panicked. We called up our friend Greg at U.S. Biofuels in Georgia. He had been producing during the good times, and had retooled his family's chemical plant over to biodiesel. He was a big producer. He explained that the solution to our problem was simple. "Switch to poultry fat," he said. And so we bought a load of poultry fat.

Which brought our plant to its knees. We had to shut down, and re-plumb, and re-invest, and change our recipe, and change our catalyst, and at long last we beat poultry fat into submission.

We didn't know it at the time, but I believe we were the third plant on earth to figure out how to spin chicken fat into fuel. Greg was the first. I remember eating lunch with some folks at the National Biodiesel Board conference in the winter of 2007, and when I told them we were running on poultry fat they said, "You can't do that."

Poultry fat eventually headed the way of soybean oil, in that it became too expensive to turn into biodiesel. We began the cut over to waste vegetable oil in the dead of winter, and like the change to poultry fat, it ground our plant to a halt. Poultry fat was tough, but used cooking oil was spotty. It would arrive at the plant gate full of water and chunks and produced assays that we were not accustomed to. And our production faltered.

Profits eluded us again.

And while many of our undertakings "worked," many of them took too long. Because we are wedded to doing everything ourselves, we tend to be slower, and we tend to pay a lot of "tuition" along the way.

We don't hire seasoned professionals. We hire interns. Passionate people like us. Who make mistakes, and pay dearly to learn.

Our financial picture looked grim in the late winter of 2007 when suddenly a European oil company arrived at our doorstep with a desire to "toll" our plant. Tolling operations are not uncommon in the chemical industry, and the arrangement is simple.

The "tolling" entity buys all of the feedstocks, and for that matter all the liquids in the plant, and the company doing the work simply gets paid a processing fee.

On the surface it appeared that with this arrangement we would be insulated from the vagaries of the global commodity markets, and we took to it readily. Finally we were safe from rising feedstock costs and needed only to work our magic by spinning fat into fuel.

That went well for a while. Suddenly our investment had promise for the first time in its life. Fat arrived on time, fuel went out the gate, and we were both amazed and proud of the thing we had built. We put on a weekend shift. Every other day a full tanker of biodiesel left the plant when we were at peak stride.

One obvious problem with the relationship was that the oil company was shipping everything to Rotterdam. Here is the way it worked:

They leased a multi-million-gallon tank in a deep harbor, and sent trucks to our facility. Their tank had a floating lid. Each time we filled a truck with 7700 gallons of fuel, we raised the lid by one inch. A day and a half of our human endeavor raised the lid by one inch.

Once they had aggregated enough biodiesel to fill a supertanker, they would steam to Rotterdam, where most liquid fuels enter the European Union. There our poultry-fat-derived biodiesel would be blended with rapeseed-derived biodiesel, and from there it would be blended into petroleum diesel, and from there it would be shipped into EU countries.

At the time it seemed like a minor transgression. After all, US oil companies and consumers were not buying our expensive, low carbon fuel. Europeans were. Here we had spent years on the journey to make sustainable biodiesel, and that was indeed what we were pumping into our cars and trucks in the yard, but by the time it made it to London Town, the poor chap filling up with a blend of biodiesel made in Pittsboro, North Carolina could not really call himself "green."

When we were tolling we were cash positive. Everyone got paid on time. And we were making a lot of fuel. Looking under the covers we realize now that really it was the collapse of the American dollar that made the relationship work. Our customer was paying in Euros as the American dollar went down the drain.

At that point Germans were shopping in Manhattan, and street vendors in New York City started accepting Euros. We had

Europeans shopping for real estate on the Pittsboro-Moncure Road. It was a wild time. For Europeans, America was 50% off, and even fuel made from local chicken fat could be shipped across the ocean at a profit.

Our own profit picture looked promising in the fall of 2008, before the Euro, and then the global economy crashed. In September I stood on a mountain of cash, looking out on a profit for the year — our first profitable year ever. And by November it was over.

About that time my beloved brother and business partner Mark fell ill with cancer.

At Piedmont Biofuels he was our comedian, and our financial engineer, and our "no" man.

Mark and I had been entangled in various business ventures together for over twenty years. Our relationship was somewhat "spousal" in nature. I would either meet with him, or call him several times a day, and on evenings and weekends we would get together to party, or chop wood, or hang out together. He was my "big brother," and by any definition we were tight as could be. I did the vision, he did the work, and together we built significant enterprises.

As Mark lay dying in a hospital in Chapel Hill, I stopped minding the store. I spent my waking hours in waiting rooms and in the Intensive Care Unit, and I snatched some time at home with the boys, and I would sometimes visit the biodiesel plant that was adrift.

Our administration was coming unglued, our leadership was absent, and the global recession was upon us. By the time Mark asked me to retrieve his living will from his bedroom closet, Piedmont Biofuels was a goner.

I buried my partner. My best friend. And my daily companion. And in exchange he left me as both the executor, and beneficiary of his estate.

When I returned to Piedmont, in the complete fog of grief, we were in even worse financial shape than ever before. And I spent 2009 propping up the company with remnants from Mark's estate.

Mark trusted me with all he had created, and I tried to be mindful of that. Mark used to refer to putting more money into Piedmont as "putting lipstick on a pig." At the same time I know that all Mark wanted was to see us succeed, so I embraced that task as well. Failing because of the absence of money did not seem right to me. And so I dumped my share of Mark's estate into the project.

Meanwhile, the world commodity markets began to surge, and the issue of food vs. fuel gained traction in the public eye.

Despite the fact that the biodiesel industry always loses whenever it bids on fats, oils, and greases with which to make fuel (the food industry always wins the bidding), the biodiesel industry is not without sin.

Greed has a way of burning down rainforests in Indonesia to plant oil palm trees all in a row. Harvest the oil-rich palm seeds, squish them into oil, put the oil on a supertanker to America, spin it into fuel in the Seattle harbor, put it on a train to North Carolina, then truck it to the Raleigh Durham Airport Authority and give them an award for being "green."

I've addressed the food vs. fuel issue many times in blog entries and articles. Perhaps the most comprehensive was at the Virginia Military Institute on the last day of March in 2009. This is what I wrote for the readers of Energy Blog:

Blog

Next Generation Biofuels: Origins, Myths and Outcomes

Tomorrow I am speaking at the Virginia Military Institute. And no, it is not an April Fool's joke. I intend to drop the boys at school, drive to VA, and give this talk.

I should note that I stopped publishing my speeches a long time ago. Because I stopped writing them. And there is a lot of redundancy. I give about a talk a week, and as long as it is about sustainable biodiesel, I am to the point of just walking on stage, and laying it down. I didn't even use notes at the National Biodiesel Board in February.

But Next Generation is new for me. I don't usually get tapped for that. And so I wrote it out. And I will give it the old fashioned way. Here is what I am going to say:

Before I launch into a talk on the "Next Generation," I should note that I am a "First Generation" guy. I've been making biodiesel since 2002, I've been to every National Biodiesel Board Conference since they started staging conferences, and so I am what you would call a "pioneer."

I believe that if you do a Wikipedia search on "Pioneer," it might be defined as the guy with the arrows in his back.

I started making biodiesel for my tractor out of left over cooking oil from deep fried turkeys. I threw my hat into the ring with Leif and Rachel and we formed Piedmont Biofuels as a cooperative fuel making venture together.

The Coop was well received and has about 500 members and currently powers a bunch of local families with fuel made from waste vegetable oil that is collected from area restaurants. By some accounts it is the largest biodiesel cooperative on the continent, and we certainly have a large community of people who drive around on 100% biodiesel.

Our history is very simple. It began with making fuel from waste. People thought that was cool and started showing up looking for some. When Rachel and I got our first ten-gallon batch to separate, I think there were six people standing around clapping. Everyone gets a gallon and a half to go home on.

It doesn't take long before you need more fuel than you can make. So what did we do? We built a terminal so we could buy fuel from far away and distribute it to those who wanted some.

Which means we built fueling infrastructure. In the Research Triangle Park of North Carolina, there are eight locations where you can buy 99.9% biodiesel. We call it the B100 Community Trail and it actually stretches from Wilmington on the coast to Asheville in the mountains — owned and operated by a variety of companies along the way.

Want to run around on alternative fuels? Great. Build the infrastructure to make it possible. Those of you who are backyard brewers know the scene. Lifting a five-gallon carboy to fill your tank takes some strength.

The idea was to build a "community scale" plant that would meet the fueling needs of our community. It turned out a million gallons was a little too big — forcing us to sell fuel elsewhere.

We've sold product in the domestic market, and we've sold product to Korea, and we've sold product to Europe, and we are back to selling product locally. All of our customers are oil companies. And we've been kicked around some.

We took a page out of *Goldilocks and the Three Bears*. Our Coop biodiesel plant was too small. Our Industrial biodiesel plant was too big. And nowadays we are busy shipping biodiesel plants all over the place. They are fleet scale, or farm scale, or pilot scale, and they are what I would call just right.

And now apparently biofuels will be OK as long as they are Next Generation.

I've been quirky. I've been sexy. I've been evil. I'm really not that Next Generation.

But the reason the world has turned to Next Generation Biofuels is because the first generation broke our hearts. It did this a couple of ways. The first was energy balance. When we calculate the number of fossil BTUs that go into making a gallon of biofuel we become extremely interested in how many renewable BTUs come out. And if that energy balance is low, let's not waste our time on biofuels.

The second was food. If the average American consumes 3000 calories a day (suffering from fat ankles and affluenza), and it takes 30K calories to fill an SUV with ethanol, biofuels look like a rotten idea.

Perhaps the "Food vs. Fuel" debate was simply a plot by the grocery lobby. That's what our trade association would have you believe. Or perhaps it shined a light on the idea that we need new pathways to biofuels.

If you take the seed of the corn plant, which is full of starch, and you convert that starch to sugar, you can ferment that sugar into alcohol and use it for motive power. If that corn was supposed to go into a tortilla to feed a hungry child in Mexico, but instead helped you make another pointless trip to the mall on the edge of town, we have a problem.

If you take the fat from a soybean, and convert it into biodiesel, you can use that to get around too. But if we live in a hungry world that is short on fat, and if we use a whole lot of petroleum to raise that fat from the earth, biofuels don't look so hot.

So biofuels are "maybe not so good."

As a society we have decided that instead of drawing a line through biofuels, we will instead look toward the "Next Generation."

The thinking is that if we can get out of the seed, and into the stalk, all will be well. The premise is that in the next generation we will make alcohol from cellulose rather than from starch. People get to eat the seed, and cars will consume the stover.

At this point we are unclear as to whether or not the stover may be a necessary ingredient to provide health to the soil. Soil can be a renewable resource. If we treat it right. And it could very well be that treating the soil right is more important than deriving fuels from the biomass left over from our crop harvests.

In order for ethanol to get a get-out-of-jail-free card, it needs to distance itself from its current production methods. Its energy balance is deemed too low, and it successfully competes with food. So the "Next Generation" will come from cellulose.

Give it a few years.

It will get there from here. In the absence of conservation. And public transportation. And sidewalks. And in the absence of bike lanes. And in the absence of logic, the Next Generation of biofuels will be made from something else and all will be well.

Something to note is that the biosphere cannot possibly grow enough BTUs to power this current wasteful economy. Conversations about biofueling the future are meaningless in the absence of total and complete changes to the ways we consume fuel. Conservation first. Then fuel.

Biodiesel is in the same boat as ethanol for its next generation. What we like to do in biodiesel is differentiate ourselves from ethanol.

When it comes to producing fat for biodiesel the Next Generation conversation moves to brand new feedstocks. Instead of soybeans we talk about jatropha. Instead of palm oil we talk about moringa. One of the things we trumpet is a crop that will grow on "marginal land." Since we got into trouble with the environmentalists for burning the rainforest and planting oil palm trees all in a row, we came up with the marginal land argument. The reality is that we get more oil per acre on fertile land than we do on marginal land, so we tend to plant our new oil seed crops on the best land available.

Biodiesel runs into lots of Next Generation problems. Jatropha, for instance, is toxic. In the developing world it is used for abortions. Once we squish the oil out of the seed, what are we going to do with the mountain of toxic meal that is left behind?

Next Generation for biodiesel generally spells algae. The simple explanation is that algae reproduce so rapidly that the "oil per acre" yield is out of this world. But whenever someone plays the algae card, make sure you count trump. Algae is a *kingdom*. It is like saying we will make biofuels from trees. Some have sap. Others have tar. Some lose their leaves. Others stay green.

There are lots of varieties of algae in the world. Some make oil. Some do not. Some are so hydrophilic you can't get the water out. Most need to be stressed by diet to even make oil in the first place.

The idea that we are simply going to drive around on biofuels derived from algae is a long way out.

One of the things the industry misses about fuel from algae is that cultivating it is like cultivating any livestock. It takes water, and nutrients, and has weed and predation pressures like anything else. And it gives off wastewater, like any livestock.

Algae is not a free lunch. Nothing is, in the energy business. Regretfully the laws of thermodynamics regulate us.

For me the Next Generation of biofuels will come from drilling deeper into the waste stream. Today we are making biodiesel from agricultural fats. Tomorrow those fats will be used for their intended purpose first, and then used for biodiesel. We will be making fuel from fats that have gone down the drain. Tomorrow we will be making fuels from crop residues rather than crops.

Down in North Carolina we have a Biofuels Center. It is a remarkable campus, with state funding, and a bunch of big-brained folks who are working on building an industry. They have a mission from the North Carolina legislature, and they are feverishly working on getting biofuels into our state's liquid fuel mix.

Their president is Steven Burke, and I love to listen to him talk, because he routinely transcends the details in which I am immersed. He doesn't talk about miscanthus, or switch grass or biodiesel. When he speaks of biofuels he uses words like "imperative," "urgency," "responsibility," and "vision."

And he is right. When it comes to any generation of biofuels it is less about *how* than it is about *why*. Why is because fossil fuels face depletion. Why is because America has grown dependent on fuel from countries who don't really care for us. Why is because our climate is changing in ways that are detrimental to our species.

We have to figure this out, folks.

Along the way we will take arrows in the back. And we will knock up against some myths. And we will innovate, and we will labor, and we will experiment, and we will find a way...

By the fall of 2009 the industry was bruised and battered, and Piedmont was an empty shell, from a financial standpoint. At the time almost 80% of the biodiesel industry in America was shuttered. Or producing at a fraction of its capacity. Everyone was limping. High feedstock costs and low fuel prices crippled us.

I should note that financial performance is but one measure of a company. As a place, and as a culture, by almost any other measure, Piedmont was doing wonderfully. Mark Anielski, author of *The Economics of Happiness,* characterizes "genuine wealth" with a balanced, five-pointed star. He states that the proper balance of human capital, social capital, natural capital, built capital, and financial capital is needed for the formation of happiness.

Piedmont Biofuels, and its staff, fared very well when held up against Anielski's thinking. From a human capital standpoint, we are wealthy beyond our dreams. We are packed with extremely talented and bright people who are on a mission to change the world. Long hours, low pay, anything to learn, adapt, and change. Unbelievable people. Our human capital is so high that I feel slow-witted in the company of many of the people on our project.

Our social capital is a little different. In the world of grassroots sustainable biodiesel, we are rock stars and our social capital is quite high. In the world of Pittsboro, North Carolina, it varies. Part of our community loves what we are attempting to do, and part of it holds us in contempt. Generally, though, we would receive high marks for social capital, too.

For the time being our natural capital is off the charts. We live in the woods, surrounded by rivers and streams and a giant lake around which there is zero development.

Built capital is our problem. We have way more built capital than we can afford. We built an amazing biodiesel plant, and an amazing farming operation, and a remarkable eco-industrial park.

But as a point on our star it might throw us out of balance. Using a facility that can churn out a million gallons of fuel a year to make 10K gallons a month seems out of balance.

And while we might get high marks for built capital, it has taken all of our financial capital to get there.

So our star is lopsided.

Some folks would argue that a failure on the financial front is a failure on the only front that matters. Others would argue that Piedmont's success in the world lies in what it has demonstrated.

At one of our management meetings in the fall of 2009 I asked Rachel, one of our co-founders, "If Piedmont closed tomorrow would you call it a failure?"

"Absolutely not," was her answer.

That said, our failure to make a profit has made for an insane scramble to keep our doors open. We brought in some grants, and we re-financed, and we mortgaged stuff, and we re-mortgaged stuff, and we struggled month in and month out.

In the fall of 2009, after six years of tough slogging, three days before our annual Piedmont Halloween party, I was without a costume idea. Don't ask me why Halloween parties are so huge at Piedmont. They just are.

I was anxious about my lack of imagination when my friend Matt Rudolf approached me and said, "Why don't you just give up? Look at you, don't you know when you are beat?"

His comment rekindled the flame within. I took my thick purple hooded bathrobe to the embroidery shop and had Piedmont's logo stitched on the back in bright yellow and green letters. I borrowed some boxing gloves, and I showed up as a prizefighter.

I have frequently told our staff that we are not out of the fight. It might be the fifth round, and we might have a cut over our eye, and we may have lost the use of our left hook, but it is a scheduled twelve round fight.

We can still win this.

That same month Piedmont was $10,000 short on making payroll. We had until Friday to click the button on our automatic payroll plan. We sanitized our accounts receivable, we watched the mail daily, and on exactly the last day a $14,000 check arrived from the IRS for our blender's credit. Thanks to production, everyone was paid on time.

November was a different story. On the third week of November, we had $1,000 cash on hand. We gathered the entire company around and explained that if this was payday, we could split it fifteen ways.

Leif and Jeremy managed to fill the terminal with fuel from feedstocks Moya and Russell had collected, and they shipped the first full load we had shipped for awhile. The oilman who bought it, Brian Potter, a cautious supporter of our project, prepaid at our request. Brian's money came as a huge relief. Everyone would get half a paycheck.

At the same time, David and his crew from design-build finished up the biodiesel plant they had installed at Starworks in Star, North Carolina, and their executive director, Nancy agreed to pay on the spot.

On the day payroll was due I called her up and offered to bring her lunch. She said she had brought her own lunch.

I suggested that I bring her dessert.

She said, "I think what you need is a check. Bring me some beer and we will talk about it."

So Tami and I drove to Star, with a six-pack of Angry Angel, made at the Big Boss brewery in Raleigh. We had some beers with Nancy, and came home with enough money for everyone to get paid.

What I found astounding about that October and November is that even in the face of complete disaster, with complete transparency about our financial condition, no one left their post. No one quit. Everyone dug in.

At one point in a company-wide meeting Bruce said, "Hell, if we ain't goin' to get paid we might as well just go over there and do some work." In the same meeting Moya said, "I don't have a mortgage. If there is money, you can give my share to David so he can get his mortgage paid."

She was ready to go without. But not ready to leave the project.

It was remarkable. For a moment there our employees financed us.

The first quarter of 2010 saw us turn a corner. Leif had left his desk in the Control Room in the fall, donned a uniform, and started operating the plant. He figured out the ballet and ramped production up to the point where we could ship one full load to the oil industry, and keep the B100 Community Trail stocked with product.

Barely. The B100 Community Trail is a series of "stations" where Coop members can buy fuel directly. Piedmont currently operates five of these locations, with another three operated by Marc Dreyfors over at Carolina Biofuels out of Durham, North Carolina.

With production hovering at around 10,000 gallons per month, we found ourselves cash positive. The company remained in a fragile condition, but profitable fuel making gave everyone hope.

And just as we were allowing hope to creep in, we lost our $1.00 per gallon production credit from Uncle Sam. The Washington term was that the subsidy had "lapsed." The Obama administration was so busy working on climate change over in Copenhagen that they forgot to renew the subsidy that the biodiesel industry depended upon.

As an aside, $1.00 per gallon is the cheapest subsidy for any fuel in America. Petroleum is ranging about $10.00 per gallon, by the time you factor in the cost of war, and health effects, and climate change. And ethanol is running about $3.00 a gallon worth of subsidy, again, powered by petroleum- grown corn.

Conventional wisdom said the biodiesel production credit would be reinstated, and that it would be retroactive. I made a trip to Washington, to go door to door to North Carolina's congressional delegation, and I believe I did all that I could to get the message across. We did not have pockets deep enough to allow us to lose a dollar on every gallon we pumped while we waited for new legislation to arrive.

I lost that argument. The production credit expired, as did what little remained of the biodiesel industry in America. Those plants operating at limited capacity shut down entirely, and it appeared that would be Piedmont's fate as well.

Our management team met to plot strategy, and Brian Potter of Potter Oil stepped in to take every gallon we could make, allowing us to charge him an extra dollar. He was confident the credit would return, and that it would be retroactive, and he clearly had pockets deep enough to play that game.

The great irony was that when other biodiesel plants closed the price of feedstocks fell, and in February of 2010 we were able to take delivery of our first full load of feedstocks in an entire year.

We put up a solid January, February, and March and turned in the first positive quarter in the history of the project. I felt my load lightening. In late March, however, we completed our forecasts for the upcoming six months and the picture was very bleak indeed.

With an industry hobbled by the "lapsed" subsidy, our design-build business fell off a cliff. It is a business that is dependent on biodiesel producers making investments. We sell upgrades, and plant improvements, and new plants to people entering the business. That fact, combined with the end of grant funding for one of our big research and analytics projects made the next six months appear dark as ever.

As always, I searched for the good news or the positive spin, and at the time the best I could come up with was that it was merely a forecast, and that we had time to take corrective actions.

Our "capital star" was hopelessly out of balance again with the financial part worn down to the nub. We were thriving as a group, our community of impassioned believers was intact and growing but we had no money remaining.

Interestingly enough, sometimes hardship can improve your capital position. Take spills for instance. They tend to be expensive and difficult to manage but they can also have a galvanizing effect.

One of the uncomfortable aspects of running a chemical plant is that we occasionally have spills. Valves fail. Humans fail. Designs do not always account for every eventuality. The majority of our spills are contained. We have spill containment built around all of our tanks, and we comply with the Spill Prevention Control and Countermeasure (SPCC) regulations, and we advise our consulting customers how to do the same, but despite rigorous efforts and expense some spills still get away from us.

One time we had a junior plant operator park 15 thousand gallons of vegetable oil in the ditch. It was a mess. And hard to clean up. We reported it, and embarked on the difficult and expensive task of digging out the vegetable oil-soaked soil and replacing it.

Another time we had four hundred gallons of free fatty acids, which are somewhat akin to vegetable oil, pump out of our boiler room onto the driveway, run into the storm water drain and into one of our settling ponds. On that occasion we removed the grease-covered gravel, and sent it to an incinerator where the goo could be rapidly volatized and the gravel could be re-used on driveways and such. What was interesting about that spill is that they would not allow us to pile the gravel in the sun to let it naturally volatize and be re-used on our own gravel road.

After replacing the gravel, and cleaning the ditch and culverts, we set about vacuuming free fatty acids off the top of the pond.

The day we attacked the pond we had one set of hip waders, which fit me fine, and I got a lesson from Moya on how to suck grease off the top of water.

I spent the day in the pond, with a PVC stinger draped over my shoulder, gingerly vacuuming up the top surface of the pond. It was unusual. Our design-build guys came to the water's edge and devised a boom that they could drag across the water to pull the grease closer to the point of vacuum.

People pitched in with buckets, and others worked the boom, and as we all managed the vacuum truck, the spill gradually went away. We loaded the whole thing into one of our "wash" tanks and put heat to it such that the water would drop out quickly.

It was a long day. What we didn't realize when we embarked on tackling the daunting task was the way it would pull us all together. We couldn't have asked for a better problem to solve on a "corporate retreat."

Retreats cost money. In the past I have hired facilitators and paid for mileage and rooms and bar tabs. They are not cheap.

I'm not suggesting that everyone have a spill in order to have a low cost corporate retreat, but it did pull everyone together, and it did increase morale and we did solve the problem ourselves — which is sort of the Piedmont way.

And as always, it brought us closer to our friends in the regulatory community.

In Bed with Government

WHEN THE "ECONOMIC DOWNTURN" struck in the fall of 2008, a new vocabulary arose from our state and federal governments. We started hearing about "stimulus money," and "recovery funds," and Uncle Sam seemed to take a newfound interest in "Green Collar Jobs."

Early on, before any program had been designed or implemented, Bill Wilcox, a reporter from the *Chatham News and Record*, called the control room where I work and asked if the stimulus package would be good for Piedmont Biofuels.

I had no idea. I didn't even know what a stimulus package was. But I said, "Yes. Piedmont Biofuels is in the perfect position to create jobs in the new economy." And he ran a story with a headline that said something like, "Stimulus Money to Help Piedmont," and that was that.

As the recession deepened I started trundling off to workshops and conferences on how to access the vast pots of money that were being bandied about.

We never entered the renewable fuel business with an eye toward grants. To be honest, I don't even like grants. Not only are they a lot of trouble to write, they tend to be painful to administer, and they bring government into the business as a partner.

I like some people in government. And I would welcome them into our affairs and business. And others I could do without. Some are clumsy and slow-witted and fat and happy, and seldom does government ever possess the sense of urgency that is a hallmark of our project.

In *Biodiesel Power* I wrote at length about "Our Friend Grant," and how no sooner had we embarked on our journey into renewable fuel than voices began to clamor, "You should get a grant for that."

We were reluctant. But we climbed into bed with the North Carolina State Energy Office, and the North Carolina Solar Center, and the North Carolina Department of Environment and Natural Resources, Division of Air Quality. And in no time we found ourselves in the grants business.

I think that is a fair description. Entering the world of grants, or public monies, we found it to be a strange and complex place. On the surface it appears to work like this:

A government agency releases a Request for Proposal (RFP). They outline what they would like to see happen with the money, and invite suitors to line up with great ideas. Winners tend to be the ones who can match ideas closest to the RFP. And repeat winners tend to be the folks who get the money, and deliver on what they said they were going to do.

We began our grant writing days by shooting way wide of the net, and as time progressed we tightened our aim. We also learned that grants don't really come from agencies. They come from people. Which means to be successful in the world of grants, you really need to know everyone in charge of giving the money away.

The reality is that most of the money which flows from government to industry is usually going to the ideas of industry in the first place. This has helped us, since we have long been a generator of new ideas for the economy, and this has hurt us, since it means that many grant solicitations are already destined to one company or another before the RFP even arrives in our mailbox. As we became more experienced, we learned to dodge those proposals that were not really competitive grants in the first place.

Piedmont went from being a newcomer to a strong competitor in the world of grants. We figured it out, learned the business, and now we do it reasonably well. Time and again we have demonstrated our ability to be a good steward of public money. We do what we say we are going to do. We survive the audits. We file our reports on time. And perhaps more importantly, we generate ideas and projects that are on the edge of where society is currently standing, presumably where it wants to go.

That is not to say we win every time. One time we came up with the notion of "rent the oil," in which someone would build a crushing plant, create food grade oil, rent it to restaurants, collect it after it had been used, and convert the used cooking oil into biodiesel. We dreamt up the plan, and were delighted to see a solicitation arrive from the Biofuels Center of North Carolina — a private nonprofit for which I serve on the board — that was inviting people to submit an idea for a "round trip cooking oil to biodiesel project."

We were delighted to see our idea in the world, we worked up a competitive bid, and we lost it to our friend Jeremy and the good people at Appalachian State University in Boone, North Carolina.

Piedmont is often called upon to write "Letters of Support" for those taking a run at one pot of money or another. And we ask the same. When Jeff and Dennis and Jeremy win one up in Boone, we tend to cheer — to think the idea will come to pass — rather than to curse the fact that we "lost."

The same is true on the federal level. The only difference is that the pond is bigger, and the pots of money are larger. But the fix is often in. I've read federal solicitations that specify what the "successful candidates" will possess. Something like: they will have a minimum of a million acres of soybeans under contract, and a 60 million gallon per year crushing facility with adjoining biodiesel plant. Hmmm. Looks like Cargill is the only company that need apply for that one.

If I were jaded and bitter about the world of grants — which I try not to be since I would like to give government a chance — I would suggest there is a link between giant federal grant solicitations and campaign finance. Those who are more conspiracy minded than me like to suggest that the grants begin with a run for office. Corporate America funds the candidate, and when the candidate wins, he or she selects company officials to help them serve, and the next thing you know there are grant solicitations on the street that only certain companies need apply for.

I want to believe that government is trying to do the right thing, and that there is no quid pro quo although sometimes I wonder. And I think it is true that government is often all thumbs when it comes to administering grants properly.

One of the reasons I say this is that government does not move at the speed of business. Decision making is slower. It has to be, I suppose, in order to preserve transparency, and to follow the cumbersome rules associated with the public purse. Because grant money is so slow, it often arrives long after the business problem it was designed to address is gone.

I'm convinced that you can't run a business based on grants. If you do, you will find yourself opening, and closing, opening, and closing as the cycles of grants occur and as the well-meaning bureaucracy figures out how to deliver the money without getting fired or engulfed in scandal.

By the fall of 2009 Piedmont Biofuels had been awarded $339,000 worth of government grants — much of which was from stimulus money. That means a lot of press releases had been sent out, a lot of speeches had been made, and the public perception was that Piedmont was rolling in cash.

I once had a call from Nancy at Starworks, and she started the conversation by saying, "I hear you have been stimulated."

We had just won an award from the Department of Energy to continue some of the work we had been doing in enzymatic biodiesel production. It was a Small Business Innovation and Research (SBIR) grant, and when the news broke that we had been selected, Senator Kay Hagan's office sent out a press release that traveled throughout the pond like a lightning bolt. From the headlines, it looked like Piedmont was in good shape.

Nothing could have been further from the truth. Each month we were playing chicken with our payroll. And each month we could have been saved by any number of grants that were slotted to come our way.

By December of 2009 I was so fed up with not having received one penny of stimulus money, I went to DC to attempt to round up some political pressure. I would hear politicians discussing the new "green economy," and the urgent need to get money into the hands of businesses in the name of job creation and preservation, and while we waited for money to arrive, we kept getting smaller and smaller.

Unemployment in North Carolina was running at 11%, about 1% higher than the national average. The biodiesel portion of our project had fallen from 25 employees to 14, and was on the brink of collapse.

At the time we were fending off threats. We had one line of credit called in the credit crunch, and after covering it we were scared indeed. We started de-leveraging the business as fast as we possibly could. As our cash supplies dwindled, and our ability to borrow more capital vanished in the depression, we found ourselves threatened by vendors, and customers, and the banks, and the regulators. It takes money to stay in compliance in the chemical business, and when the money runs out, non-compliance quickly follows.

During those days I spent the lion's share of my time working on finance. It was harrowing. And the whole time I did so I knew

Senator Kay Hagan is one of the many public officials who have toured the Plant.

that we had capital commitments from government agencies that vastly exceeded what we needed to survive.

It drove me nuts. Capital markets were not interested in our money-losing enterprise, banks were preoccupied with whether or not they should return their bailout funds, and there was literally nowhere to get money.

On top of that we had been taking orders from government entities for design-build projects. We sold a biodiesel plant to Craven County Schools. They wanted it to be built on a school bus such that they could drive around with the kids, pick up used cooking oil from area restaurants, and turn it into biodiesel to power the bus and some of their landscaping equipment.

The project was perfect from a sustainability standpoint. In fact, I believe it was funded by a grant from the Biofuels Center of North Carolina. That is, the Biofuels Center funded Craven County, and Craven County used the money to buy a mobile biodiesel plant from us.

One more connection to grant money. As stimulus money started arriving at public schools, and Community Colleges, and Universities, people started calling us to build small-scale facilities for them. And unlike our usual contracts, where we collected a 50% deposit up front — to pay for things like tanks and pumps and pipes — and the "stuff" required to build the plant — the government contracts would not allow for any money down.

The way we normally run our design-build business, there is very little financing required. We get a down payment, we buy the pieces and parts and pay the labor for assembly, we typically collect progress payments when certain milestones are achieved, and we collect the final installment on completion.

With an arrangement like that, there is no bank required. The profit margin on the job is collected at the end, and all the costs have been paid for along the way.

Those operating with grant money are often not able to play by those rules. Leaving us with government purchase orders (which were presumably as good as cash), but no way to finance them.

Fortunately we drummed up some patient capital from a pair of neighbors in Green Level, North Carolina. They had a 1,000 gallon biodiesel tank in their yard, which they used to make bulk purchases. And they liked what they saw when visiting Piedmont. Together they formed the Green Level Sustainability Fund, and lent it to Piedmont against our government contracts with an agreement to let us pay the interest in fuel.

That loan was patient capital, and it arrived just in time to let us finish some lucrative government contracts. One of the great ironies of the Green Level Sustainability Fund is that it was created by libertarians. They are the folks who are convinced that government needs to get out of the way of commerce in general.

I'm conflicted about that. Part of me feels that socialism is the only way to go. America is so wasteful; with everyone sitting around on vast assets they don't share, that it makes me believe shared assets is the path to sustainability. And part of me wants to join the libertarians the first chance I get.

It often strikes me that we have made our world so confusing, so corrupt, and so impossible to navigate that I am ready to join the first person who agrees to wipe the white board of government clean to start over.

When I returned from my DC lobbying trip my efforts on Capitol Hill were greatly appreciated by my peers in the industry, and by our trade association, the National Biodiesel Board, but my efforts were far too little, too late.

None of us want to be at the trough of government largesse. None of us want to live in grant land. We embarked on a voyage of discovery, and business was our platform. Not public money.

We set out to make a profit, and pay taxes when the need arose. We did not set out to be propped up by government handouts.

I once rode across the lake with BJ Lawson, a friend of mine who once ran for congress against incumbent David Price. As we were driving I took a cell call, and it was good news indeed. The North Carolina Green Business Fund, which was administered by the North Carolina Department of Commerce had elected to award us $75,000 to expand our fabrication capabilities. We wanted to buy a metal break, and a lathe, and some other stuff to make us more competitive on the fabrication front.

For me it was good news. We received a grant announcement from the state that would allow us to be more effective at completing our mission. BJ snorted.

"So you get state money to do the things in Pittsboro that you used to pay someone in Asheboro to do," he said with disdain.

And he was right about that.

What neither of us knew at the time was that the money would not be delivered on time. If ever. I started working on getting the money in earnest in the fall of 2009 as the leaves were starting to turn. As the daffodils emerged in the spring of 2010 I still did not have a penny. Better to have not awarded it at all.

We didn't write the RFP. We merely submitted a winning proposal. But in the larger scope of things, the award did little to improve economic development for North Carolina. In BJ's view it was the perfect reason to burn government to the ground.

And while he is hard to argue with (he's a brain surgeon turned entrepreneur), we could make the case that this round of state money represented a further investment in our technology, and that would improve our prospects for commercialization and that would be a good thing for North Carolina.

And it is true that we once received a grant from the NC Green Business Fund and with it we commercialized a cavitational biodiesel reactor that we then went on to sell far and wide. We sold cavitators in Georgia, and Pennsylvania, and the Dominican Republic, and in as much as our exports helped keep North Carolinians in "green jobs," it would be easy to quantify our grant money as being successfully deployed.

So BJ is right that the government should not be in the grant making business, and we are right to vie for our share of the government grant making pie.

Deciding to jump into bed with government is a tough decision. Especially when you are happily married to free enterprise.

The reality is that enterprise isn't really free. Especially not in the energy business. Whether it is the coal-fired electrons that come across our regulated utility grid, or the crude oil that our troops escort out of the Strait of Hormuz, the price of energy does not reflect its actual cost. Whether it is a per-gallon subsidy, or a feed-in tariff, or a regulatory requirement, the cost of production is a function of government. We can't be the only energy business to operate without government policy support — which means Piedmont Biofuels would be foolish not to climb into bed with government. We are an enterprise that pushes the edge of how human beings might sustain life on this planet, and as long as we are going to be on that edge, we are wedded to government money to help with research, to deploy technology, and to continue to work on finding the low carbon future that our planet desperately needs.

One of the grants that came our way serves as a micro model for the whole grant making space. Rural Advancement Foundation International (RAFI) is a global nonprofit that is dedicated to strengthening rural communities. Part of their funding comes from tobacco settlement money — that is money awarded to state government by the courts as punishment for the tobacco industry's egregious behavior. The money is earmarked in part to help tobacco dependent counties reinvent their economies in a world where the tobacco industry is no longer. (As an industry, tobacco is alive and well in other parts of the world, it has merely moved out of the United States where the courts frowned upon its crooked ways).

The industry's departure left North Carolina with a big pot of money, and a lot of farmers and haulers and auctioneers and trades people without a livelihood. And so they decide to "grant" out that money to projects that can help rural communities reinvent themselves. A whole lot of money went into a 30 million gallon biodiesel project in Mount Olive that never got off the drawing board, and gave biodiesel in North Carolina a black eye. When people see government money going to projects that don't get built they become suspicious of why the government would even put money into biodiesel in the first place.

Some of the money ended up in the care of RAFI. A couple of times each year RAFI invites farmers and rural organizations to "compete" for money to implement projects in their communities — presumably in the name of getting something built that works.

One such proposal came from Denise at Farm Inc., a new non-profit that was focused on greenhouse growers, and Denise had a wonderful idea. She was going to take the glycerin co-product from a biodiesel plant and burn it in a boiler to heat a greenhouse. The idea was to reduce heating costs to allow greenhouse operators to be more profitable. Perfect application.

At the time we had spent six months perfecting a boiler application that took the free fatty acids from the co-products of biodiesel production and converted them into valuable heat. Denise and I got to talking. What I had was a biodiesel plant, and a way to generate co-products, and boilers up and running. I discouraged her from using the glycerin from the process since glycerin gives off a toxic carcinogen when not incinerated properly, and in our experience, boilers are imperfect incinerators.

I invited her to Piedmont, and openly agreed to share everything I knew.

What Denise had was a good idea. And a grant. And a greenhouse operator who was willing to give it a try.

We also had a greenhouse operator in the form of Screech, and he was in the middle of a large expansion.

I sat down with RAFI, and Farm Inc., and my design-build guys, and Screech, and we hatched a plan for part of the grant money to go into district heating for Screech's project.

The question then becomes whether or not this project would be a good use of public money. The system required to burn free fatty acids is custom-built; off-the-shelf boiler systems will not work. If government is interested in promoting business as usual, they should not put a dime into a custom boiler project for an individual greenhouse operator. But if they want change, it might be a good investment.

Asking RAFI to share some of the risk of a new greenhouse heating system, on the chance that it will have an impact on greenhouse operators everywhere seemed to me like the perfect use for public money. RAFI and Farm Inc. agreed, and Screech and Piedmont undertook the construction of the system. And, in light of the thousands of visitors we have each year, there is a high likelihood that other greenhouse operators will follow suit. Which will move a less expensive fuel into rural North Carolina, which will improve the odds of growers achieving profitability, thereby keeping RAFI on mission.

I think it is fair to say that all of the grants we have received fall into that category. Motivations differ. Those agencies tasked with improving regional air quality have targeted grants at biodiesel in order to help the industry come into being. Those focused on agriculture have done the same.

Our famous Small Business Innovation Research (SBIR) award for enzymatic biodiesel research came in the name of science. Normally when we make biodiesel we also make a bunch of soaps, and normally the industry washes soaps out of the fuel with water. Making biodiesel with enzymes does not produce soaps. Which means there is a chance we could eliminate water from the process. Using enzymes could also expand the types of feedstocks the industry could use — allowing us to convert crummier oils into valuable fuel. To try it, then, is in the best interest of the Department of Energy. If one of their goals is to reduce America's dependence on foreign sources of fuel, it would seem that risking some money on a brand new way to make biodiesel makes a lot of sense.

I suppose the argument could be made that government could simply do the work itself, and it should be noted that it does that too. Much of the science the US biodiesel industry depends on comes from places like the National Renewable Energy Lab (NREL) in Colorado. They do real work. And the work they do finds its way into the world.

In our mixed economy, the role of government is difficult to tease out of the role of industry. Government regulates us, offers us science, buys from us, and occasionally funds our endeavors. From the beginning of time I would estimate that Piedmont has been roughly 25% funded by grants. That number would have been closer to 12% before 2009 came along and the notion of stimulus was reinvented.

Like industry, government places bets on everything from technology to science to economic development. And thus far, a lot of government money has been bet on us.

Part of me thinks this same system is what despoiled planet Earth in the first place. Government in bed with industry poisoned our air and water and soil and defiled our nest to the point of threatening the long-term viability of the species.

I find it easy to agree with Van Jones. He was Obama's Green Collar Job Czar who abruptly left the administration in the fall of 2009. In their Sustainable World Sourcebook, the folks at the Sustainable World Coalition offer up a Van Jones quote from his book *The Green Collar Economy*:

> If all we do is take out the dirty power system, the dirty power generation in a system, and just replace it with some clean stuff, put a solar panel on top of this system, but don't deal with how we are consuming water, we don't deal with how we are treating our sister-and-brother species, we don't deal with toxins, we don't deal with the way we treat each other...If that's not part of this movement, let me tell you what you will have; you'll have solar powered bulldozers, solar powered buzz saws, and bio-fueled bombers and we'll be fighting wars over lithium for batteries instead of oil for the engines, and we'll still have a dead planet.
>
> This movement is deeper than a solar panel. Don't stop there! We're gonna change the whole thing. We are not going to put a new battery in a broken system. We want a new system! We're gonna change the whole thing.

Part of me wants to heed his advice.

And part of me reflects on the positive outcomes the system has achieved in my lifetime. We've seen a diminishment in acid rain by getting sulfur out of the air. We banned CFCs and not only stopped the destruction of the ozone layer, but now see it beginning to heal itself. Air quality has improved in my 47 years on the planet. The same system that allows greedy industrial interests to externalize their costs and pocket the profit also devises corrections, as needed, and has demonstrated an ability to lift not only our human condition, but also the condition of our environment.

Which means I am decidedly unclear about whether the system needs to be destroyed and rebuilt, or whether we can work within it. We have some anarchists on the edge of our project, which don't vote, and do nothing to contribute to civic life. Civil society, as they see it, is in such need of a radical makeover that they cannot be bothered.

And we have another group that despises America's "two-party system." They believe the system is rotten to the core, and vote for "third-party candidates." Still others see this as akin to throwing their votes away, or worse yet, helping to elect the enemy.

Which means we have three groups of believers on our project. The anarchists who are working toward their own civil society, the "third party" crowd who hopes to elect candidates who have never been tested, and the "status quo" crowd which tends to hold its nose and vote for whoever is on the ballot.

It is impossible to tar government with a single brush. The same Department of Energy that has held up our Green Business Fund award for over a year also arranged online payments of an SBIR grant that went smoothly and efficiently. And the same Department of Energy that is charged with stimulating jobs in the economy can be a bastion of the status quo.

I was once invited by the Triangle Clean Cities Coalition to submit ideas for job creation. Rachel and I sat down and fired off a list of about a quarter million dollars — everything for laboratory gear to expand our lab business (and employ more people) to upgrades to our plant.

Word came back immediately that "Bio refining operations were ineligible." Fair enough. We opted out. By their definition that is what we are. They called back and asked us to submit again. Jobs were at stake, and they knew we created jobs so they wanted to know if we had anything in the way of "renewable fuel infrastructure." I dashed off a proposal to build a new biodiesel fueling station for 40K dollars. It was to be at Jeff Barney's five star gas station in Saxapahaw.

And it was approved.

But before we could arrange a grant contract to get started (six months after the award was "given"), DOE had a few questions. For me it was simply going to be another location of the B100 Community Trail in a hip community where we knew there was demand for our fuel. We were going to build the fueling station in a straw bale shed with south facing glazing, and we were going to equip it with photovoltaic panels. Like many of our locations it was designed to be off grid, passive solar, high percentage biodiesel.

Easy.

DOE's first pass was, "Does it need to be in a building? Is there a cheaper way to keep the fuel warm?"

Yup. I told them they could lop 10K off and use and an immersion heater from China. They were glad to hear that. All I had to do was tell Doug, the builder who was looking forward to creating a straw bale structure that he would need to find other work.

DOE then came back with, "Does it need to be solar?"

Nope. I told them they could save 10K dollars by powering the facility with coal. They were glad to hear that too. All I had to do was call Chris, the solar installer who was looking forward to putting up panels on the new facility that he would need to find other work.

Not a bad gig for a "jobs creation play." Someone at DOE was surely getting points for being such a smart shopper. No doubt they were so delighted by the money they saved the government that they ran down to Walmart to save some more for themselves.

I'm completely conflicted about being at the government's trough. Part of me wants to burn government to the ground, and part of me wants to play nice since government can be the path to societal change, and at the end of the day, that is the business we are in at Piedmont Biofuels.

Depression 2.0

I'M NOT SURE what historians will settle on for the name of the financial collapse that began in the fall of 2008. "The Great Recession" seems to be in the lead. Right up until the end the pundits and experts on the radio were saying that it is "not technically a recession," even when it was clear to everyone that the end was nigh. I laughed out loud when the housing bubble began to burst and the Bush administration came out with "the fundamentals of the economy are sound."

Not being an economist, or a rocket scientist, it seems to me that any healthy economy would be simply predicated on making things. To be concise: production. And while that idea is as old as the hills, I cannot see why none of the experts get it. It seems that everyone thinks we can shop our way to prosperity.

At some point, someone, in America, is going to have to make something. Once when Tami and I journeyed to Saxapahaw to dine at Jeff Barney's remarkable general store/gas station/whatever it might be, he served us an exquisite locally raised beef hamburger and locally raised goat burger. Because he was glad to see us he threw in a couple of servings of his famous home fries, made in duck fat. He also joined us at our table. We were dining in a booth next to the Valvoline and chainsaw lubricants.

Jeff is a daring entrepreneur. He's magnetic and charismatic and is a one-man force of nature. Our thinking is flavored by him, and his by us. And when the topic of local finance surfaced, he lit up like the pre-treated briquettes in the next aisle over.

In *Small is Possible* I told the story of a ten thousand dollar loan to Diane, the cabinetmaker who needed some relief from credit card interest. That notion, of neighbors lending to neighbors has since swelled to over three hundred and fifty thousand dollars worth of lending in our little town — and those are just the loans I know about.

The beauty of micro lending is peer pressure. In order to default you kind of have to move away. And I haven't heard of any defaults yet. I know of one borrower who filed for bankruptcy, and in doing so left the state, and the bank, and a bunch of creditors hanging, but continued to service the local note.

I have seen a lot of neighbors fail in the past year or two. There has been a whole lot of defaulting going on. None yet in the local portfolio of loans that I am aware of.

The Saxapahaw General Store is a "five Star" gas station that is part of the town's revitalization.

Jeff's enthusiasm for local finance stemmed from the fact that he "can't have a transaction with himself." He pointed out that there are lots of things he can do by himself — like pray, eat, think, talk, but his inability to have a transaction with himself makes commerce a platform that demands interactions with different people. Which means if we can get it right, we can go a long way toward healing the world in which we live.

A simpler way of thinking about Jeff is that if he had access to enough finance, he would build things. Like a new restaurant, and a biodiesel pumping station, and a butcher shop, and on and on.

As we drove away from our lunch in Saxapahaw it was hard not to marvel at the way in which the town had reinvented itself. What was once merely an abandoned hulk of a mill on the beautiful rushing Haw River has sprung to life through a series of passionate endeavors. Jeff has converted a Shell station into fine patio dining. A puppet troupe, Paper Hand Puppet Intervention, has grabbed a vast tract of abandoned studio space and brought it to life for staging their inventions. A booming farmers market has emerged. And the mill is being converted into condominiums. It's impossible to drive through Saxapahaw without feeling the new vibe, and noticing a town springing back to life. There is talk of an arts center, with a dance studio, and it is the new home of the Haw River Assembly, an environmental activist group that has been fighting for the river, throwing festivals, and celebrating the river for almost thirty years.

While it easy to think of the Saxapahaw resurgence as the collective will of a bunch of passionate people, it is also important to note so much rests with the owner of the mill. The owner of the Saxapahaw mill lets things happen. Artists can use empty space in the near term, before it is converted to revenue generating space in the long term.

Down the river in Bynum it's another story. That beautiful abandoned mill had owners that would not let anything happen. It was merely a place to put stuff they didn't use. As the years wore on, with idea after idea being turned away, the mill burned to the ground and all notions of leveraging the asset to bring the community of Bynum back to life went with it.

Further down the river in Pittsboro, Tom's mill has "partially sprung to life." It's the home of Chatham Marketplace — our amazing cooperative grocery store — and slowly but surely its space is coming to life. Today there is a maker of meads setting up shop in what was once an abandoned laboratory out back.

Few of these endeavors are what we think of as "industry." Yet all of them are. If our economy is ever going to recover, it will be by making things again. If we are not making widgets, we can remake our communities, and it is going to require all of the industry we can muster.

Oilseed Community

OILSEED COMMUNITY is a remarkable study in human habitation at the end of Bill Thomas Road. I've never lived there. I once applied for membership but was told I was "too old to fit in." At the time I had children under foot (I always seem to have children under foot), and Oilseed has never been a place for children.

And while my application may have been denied, Oilseed Community was my accidental creation.

Most of the Pittsboro-Moncure Road has been acquired by Prestonwood Development Corporation out of Cary, North Carolina — roughly 5,000 acres of woods.

The concept was simple. They were going to buy up all the land, and build their own version of the Research Triangle Park in Cary. They like Cary. And they are intent on dropping Cary on our heads. And we are not that interested in what Cary represents from an urban development standpoint. In fairness to the Town of Cary, it is a well-run southern town. It is progressive in its thinking and has led the region and country with some of its initiatives. It was one of the first communities to implement curbside pickup of used cooking oil that gets sent to Wilson, North Carolina to be spun into fuel. It built an innovative wastewater treatment plant that pelletizes its biosolids to dramatically reduce the need for land application, and it has won awards from the EPA for the miles of greenways it has instituted throughout town.

Cary is not evil. It's pretty. And fakey. It has a cutesy "Sort Of New Urbanist" feel to it. And it is a bedroom community of McMansions that holds out the promise of the unsustainable over-consumed past-life American dream.

What do you do when someone spends over a hundred million dollars and buys up all the land around you? You get an appointment, and drive across the lake to pay them a visit.

Tami and I drove to the offices of Prestonwood Development Corporation in the spring of 2007. To get there we negotiated wide boulevards of manicured lawns and stone monument signs. It was neat as a pin. Color coordinated. Everything in Prestonwood Land looks so similar it is easy to get lost.

The offices are not opulent. Just nice. And like their offices, the people are nice too. Our objective was to secure a sizeable donation to the Abundance Foundation, but it was not long into our meeting when it became clear that Prestonwood would prefer to create their own community rather than participate in ours. I believe that the owners of Prestonwood Development Corporation are legendary for their personal generosity. But on this day, the Abundance Foundation need not apply.

As we were leaving empty handed, one of their executives suggested that he did have a number of empty houses he was worried about. He wasn't sure of the address, or where they were in his five thousand acres, but he said, "They are at the end of a real funny road. It starts off paved, then it goes to gravel, then it is paved again."

And he pulled out a giant aerial map and unfurled it across the board room table.

My mind was racing. I was looking at the map as if I were a camera. High voltage power lines. Click. Abandoned rail spur.

Click. Robeson Creek. Click. I was trying to memorize aerial map features so that I could find the place.

"One of the houses is stick built, and there is a manufactured home, and a single wide and some other stuff," he said. If you wanted to borrow them, and take care of them for a few years before we are ready to bulldoze, we might be able to do something there."

Housing. Possibly free housing. I was exhilarated at the thought. At Piedmont Biofuels we have wrestled with where people might live for years. We rent rooms for interns; Piedmont Biofarm rents whole houses for farm interns. A supply of potentially free housing lit me on fire.

Tami and I sped back across the lake. I dropped her at the plant, and went in search of the location. My eighteen years on the Pittsboro-Moncure Road served me well, allowing me to find the place in less than an hour. I drove down a rutted lane, and found an abandoned stick built house, a single wide with a temporary power pole, and a manufactured home with children's toys in the yard and a confederate flag strung from a sorry pole. It appeared someone still lived there. And looking out on rolling hayfields, with a long beautiful view to the power lines, there was an abandoned speed boat on a trailer, overflowing with trash.

I drove to the plant and mustered Rachel and Leif. I got Matt on the phone. I explained that we had a chance to land some human habitation for free. Everyone dropped what he or she was doing; we rushed to the site, and unanimously agreed that this would be a good thing.

With consent behind me I called Prestonwood Development, and we ended up leasing 70 acres and five dwellings for three years, for one dollar. We would be the caretakers until the golf courses were built, and we were to provide insurance, and maintenance. The deal was struck.

I believe Prestonwood felt that if these houses were left abandoned on this remote tract, there was a threat they would become crack houses and meth labs.

Not with us around. Our chemistry is targeted at sustainability. And Oilseed Community was born.

All sorts of wonderful people moved in, and we collected rents on all the rooms. We took the rent money and put it into the Coop coffers, so that the Coop could continue the good work it was doing on its quest for sustainable biodiesel.

Suddenly real estate became a revenue stream. All told, over the years it was roughly the equivalent of a $100,000 donation. Which was huge. It not only gave us a wonderful place for people to live, but it provided cash.

I took some bruising out of the deal. Those who were hell bent on fighting Prestonwood Development accused me of being in the company's pocket. But Oilseed Community was so important to the sustenance of our project that I never felt right bashing Prestonwood. One night, after attending a horrible greenwashing event, I came home furious, and wrote a damning piece about their world view. But I never published it. Here is what I wrote:

blog

_____

Prestonwood Development is a company backed by Dr. Goodnight, the founder of the SAS Institute, which is a wildly successful software company in the Research Triangle Park of North Carolina. They hail from Cary, North Carolina, in which all the awnings on all the strip malls are the same color, and all the crepe myrtle trees are pruned to perfection. If Wikipedia did a definition of "sprawl," it would be Cary.

When Moses was alive, he had a bumper sticker on his truck that read, "Find a Cure for Cary." And when Garrison Keillor passed through town to perform a live version of his "Prairie Home Companion," he suggested Cary was an acronym for "Containment Area for Retired Yankees."

Dr. Goodnight, and his merry band of planners, bankers, and greed enthusiasts came to Pittsboro-Moncure and bought up all the land around us. They bought more land than the Research Triangle Park and are fixing to do it all again. An acquisition that large threatens our sense of place.

They are big enough, and rich enough, that they can redefine place the way they want to. If they want us to be five golf course communities, they can do that. If they need water they can truck it in from Le Bleu. If they need a highway they can simply build one.

We live beneath the specter of a redefined place.

And yet Chatham Park Investors wants us to feel at ease. In order to help us breathe easy, they brought in Timothy Beatley, PhD.

Oilseed Community is tucked in the woods at the end of a long gravel road.

He's the Teresa Heinz Professor of Sustainable Communities at the University of Virginia, who also happens to be an old college buddy of Phillip Culpepper, the lead planner for Prestonwood.

Together they booked a room at our mostly abandoned Chatham Mill (right next to Chatham Marketplace), and they got a caterer to put skewers through individual radishes, and they borrowed a sound system from the Abundance Foundation, and they put on what could quite possibly be the worst lecture on sustainable communities ever staged.

Timothy Beatley appears to be an expert on Australia. That may be why he blathered on about evaporative cooling systems in Adelaide. And urban density in Barcelona. He is clearly a well traveled expert in "place," and clearly clueless about the small southern town he was addressing.

I think it is tremendously exciting that office buildings in Sydney are purging their hot daytime air with cool nighttime air. When we do that we mold. If we open our windows the covers on our paperbacks will curl.

Our air is too moist for evaporative cooling, and with a population of 2,500 surrounded by woods, we are not quite ready for high-speed rail like they use in Madrid.

Apart from being a horrible speaker (reading the text off the slides of his PowerPoint), Dr. Beatley missed the point of Chatham County, Pittsboro, and sustainability completely. While I am confident the good people of Prestonwood Development, to whom I am beholden, would like to receive accolades for their efforts to greenwash their project, I am unable to grant them a bonus point.

If anything, tonight's display demonstrated they have no clue.

Prestonwood Development, has no claim to sustainability. They dip their toe in sustainability waters if they have to, but they wouldn't know sustainability if it bit them in the ass. Yet they have been a terrific thing for our project. We are grateful for their huge contribution.

If the only yardstick we employ is the one that measures money, we have to accept a number of facts. Preston Development is "successful." Piedmont Biofuels is a beneficiary of Preston's "success."

Preston bought at the peak of the market, and the market has since collapsed. People in these parts like to say, "It's Dr. Goodnight, it don't matter how much the market is down," but I think those people are wrong. I don't care how deep the pockets are. If a hundred million turns into sixty million, or if a dollar turns into sixty cents, it hurts no matter how many dollars you possess.

Oilseed Community could be thrown out on its ear. Bulldozers could roll tomorrow. But at the end of the day Preston needs some buyers for homes in golf course communities. Oilseed Community might be on borrowed time, but until more buyers come along, our woods are safe and sound.

In the mean time, Oilseed Community became an economic engine for Piedmont Biofuels. Monthly room rents allowed us to power mortgages, and farmland and intern housing that we would not otherwise have been able to afford.

Yet the yardstick of money is a rotten way to measure Oilseed Community. What the rents are and where they go have nothing to do with its success. Its success lies in the way humans have learned to live together.

With its shared houses, shared kitchens, shared meals across multiple houses, and all the drama that dogs and cats and possums and chickens and humans can bring to bear, Oilseed Community could perhaps be best described as accidental cohousing.

Indeed, Oilseed Community laid the foundations for a formal cohousing group that became known as Pittsboro Co-Housing.

In the fall of 2007, we invited architect Giles Blunden to visit the eco-industrial park for a private tour. He is the brain behind

Arcadia, a cohousing community in Carrboro, and he was the developer of Pacifica, another cohousing masterpiece in Carrboro.

I was familiar with both projects, and completely impressed, and I invited him to the plant in order to stretch his thinking. In my view he had neglected two important aspects in his previous projects: energy and livelihood. About 30 percent of the people in his first two projects harness some type of renewable energy. Yawn. It needs to be higher.

And many of the people who live in these cohousing projects are commuters. Surely some walk to work in Carrboro, but many spend hours a day in the car.

I brought Giles to the plant to lay out a vision of how we could build a cohousing community in Pittsboro that would use renewable energy to heat and cool the homes. I thought we should build homes with solar-powered central heat, and photovoltaic electric power with biodiesel generator backup. And I thought they should be priced such that plant workers could move in and be able to walk to work.

Sort of a mill town, without the exploitation connotations.

Giles was intrigued.

He came back to the plant kitchen to engage in conversation with all interested parties. The place was packed.

He talked for three hours straight, without a hint of fluster, fielding all questions, about all things, effortlessly. He was masterful. And wise. One of the many notions that I took away from the meeting was his idea that if a group of interested parties gets together 40 times, a community is born.

And that is underway here.

I should note, however, that our cohousing initiative is not like most. Most cohousing projects introduce the notion of what it is like to be "in community" with one another. Most introduce extensive processes to help members learn how to discuss intimate things, like money, and pets, and personal behaviors.

Thanks to Oilseed Community, and Piedmont Biofuels, we are already doing all of that. We trade amongst ourselves, and we lend to one another, and we collect rents, and interest, and do business in such a way that we are already deeply immersed in community.

Perhaps the best filter to push this story through is that of Greg. Greg came to Piedmont Biofuels as an intern from upstate New York. He was a graduate of Cornell, and is a life-long learner with a big brain.

Pulling into our project alerted the libertarian tendencies within him. He was suspicious of shared assets, and "communal" living and our cooperative approach. He hated the PLENTY, our local currency with which we paid his stipend. At the time the PLENTY could not be exchanged for dollars at Capital Bank, which meant he was severely limited to local merchants. Greg also hated our no-commuter policy, which meant if he wanted to move in with his girlfriend in Hillsborough, that was fine, he would simply not be able to work at Piedmont anymore.

At the outset, I think our approach to getting things done was jarring to Greg. Not efficient, not clearly delineated. He was a skeptic.

Greg migrated from his initial internship with us into a "senior" intern position in which he embarked on developing a used cooking oil collection business. Greg was instrumental in securing a loan from Self Help Credit Union for our first vacuum truck, and some private loans for our first collection of grease dumpsters.

Greg went on to operate our big biodiesel plant in Pittsboro, and in doing so became a founding resident of Oilseed Community. In essence, he has traveled along a spectrum, from skeptic to an avid communitarian. Greg is the one who organizes sports events, is a pillar of potlucks, and now focuses his thinking through the lens of the greater project.

The scientist in him led him into the development of Piedmont's Research and Analytics division, in which he partnered with

Rachel, who has long led our analytical efforts, and Xiaohu, our resident PhD.

Greg now has his own lab, and is fully engaged in the leading thinking on biodiesel production.

The notion that we are here for the community, and that by working together as a diverse group we might find a way to sustain human life on this planet, is a common idea that Greg and I now share.

In its current iteration, Pittsboro Co-Housing is looking at a 40-acre parcel on the other side of the fence from our eco-industrial park. It would be a multi-million dollar endeavor that would house 30–40 families.

One of the tenets of cohousing is to stay in small groups, since the human animal is only capable of sustaining intimacy with a small number of people. That is, better to do three cohousing projects of 30 than a single project of 90 units.

A handful of people from the Pittsboro Co-Housing project have expressed interest in developing a one-acre parcel that is inside the fence of our eco-industrial park. The idea is to apply to the Town of Pittsboro for a minor subdivision, so that land that is currently zoned industrial could be re-zoned for residential. This would allow five units to be built, and would entail the pulling of electrical, sewer, water, etc. to an isolated patch of woods on the edge of the plant.

The proposed location is on a gentle rise, so residents would look out on the rolling fields of Piedmont Biofarm, and on the tank farm of our chemical plant. It might not sound bucolic, but it is.

The inclusion of a farm at our eco-industrial park means that we have three acres of "vacant lots" which surround us on all sides, and those lots have been converted into beautiful beds of okra, and garlic, and peppers. They are a scenic and comforting sight all year round. For some of us, the view of a biodiesel plant gives us a sense of energy security.

I am not the least bit surprised that a small group of people would like to live inside the gates. Where they work. Inside the town limits. Where they can have a vote in their affairs.

It will be interesting to see if we can pull this one off. We would like to build an energy net-positive cohousing community out of used shipping containers on a piece of our campus so that people can have a permanent place to live. If we can include some dormitory-style housing for interns, we can go a long way toward solving the "human habitation" piece that we have wrestled with for many years.

One of the tragedies of our campus is that while today it is located on the edge of town, it is smack dab in the middle of two giant developers, both of which want to run a four-lane bypass on either side of us. If Prestonwood has their way the bypass will be to our east, and if Pittsboro Place Partners has their say it will be to our west.

Either way the value of the land we are perched on will skyrocket, and the woods that surround us will make way for the likes of Payless Shoes.

I routinely go to lunch with the developers who surround us, and the one thing no one talks about is the very real likelihood that America's economy will never recover and that Pittsboro will never explode. All of their business models assume that Depression 2.0 is merely the normal ebb of the business cycle and that one day things will return to "normal."

I'm suspicious. I believe that the horrible "downturn" of 2008–2009 might just be the beginning of our downward journey to a steady state economy. Which may seem like a contradiction — that is, if we have not yet hit bottom, why on earth would we be embarking on a housing project?

And the answer is because it will fill up immediately. Each unit will be pre-sold before it is even built. And the buyers will be those kindred souls who want to locate where they have real whole food, and renewable energy, and sustainable fuel, and a community that values the same.

9

Bringing Product to Market

AT PIEDMONT BIOFARM we are in the worm business. We sell worms. We sell worm poop (called castings in polite circles). We sell worm digesters. And we sell expertise in the form of workshops, speaking gigs, and consulting.

One of the things I love about the worm business is that it goes beyond sustainability and pushes on to rejuvenation. If we accept the notion that the human animal has done a lot of damage to this planet via its "industrial" activity, then we must recognize that we have a lot of remediation to do. And worm castings are a great start.

My wholehearted enthusiasm for worm castings actually came from some spam sent out by Bountiful Backyards in Durham, NC. They were having a "Worm Workshop," and the verbiage that preceded their advertisement suggested, "Sustainability does not go far enough. We need to rejuvenate."

I loved it. And it inspired me to bring our worm castings to market.

Our story of worms began with Brian Rosa. He moved to North Carolina from Michigan, where he was in the vermiculture business. Brian works for the North Carolina Department of Environment and Natural Resources (DENR).

To call him a bureaucrat would be unfair, since he has been in business, favors free enterprise, and has the ability to transfer enthusiasm beautifully. Before our biodiesel plant had a single pipe welded, I met with a group of state regulators of which Brian was a part.

That meeting didn't go so well. I explained to the group that I felt "state regulation" did not go far enough, was under-resourced, and inadequate, and how Piedmont Biofuels was going to vastly exceed the state regulations. I believe I was passed off as a pompous twit who had never operated a chemical plant.

But despite my initial failing with regulators, Brian emerged with a suggestion. We had a campus. We were obsessed with sustainability. We should do some worm composting.

I studied the idea and concluded that it was fascinating, and wrong-headed. At the time my focus was on finding valuable purposes for the co-products of biodiesel production. When we make biodiesel, we make glycerin, and all I cared about was using worms to convert worthless glycerin into a valuable product.

In January 2005, I wrote an entry in Energy Blog entitled "No Vermiculture Tonight." It went something like this:

── *Blog* ──────────────────────────────

Worms do eat garbage. And they convert waste into valuable castings. And there is a worm market. And there is no good role for worms at Piedmont Biofuels. Drat. I was hoping that we could toss one of our empty buildings over to a worm business, and have the worms consume the glycerin that comes out of biodiesel production.

But glycerin is mostly carbon, and worms like mostly nitrogen, and worms don't groove on greasy substances. They breathe through their skin, and while they need moisture to breathe, glycerin will suffocate them.

The king of worms, and perhaps the king of composting in general, is a fellow named Brian Rosa. He works for the Department of the Environment and Natural Resources (DENR), as an "organics" specialist.

He completed the biofuels program at Central Carolina in Pittsboro, and now sits with me on the Sustainability Advisory Board down at the College. Brian came out and toured the future home of Piedmont Biofuels Industrial with Forrest, and he set us straight on worms.

Worms need kitchen scraps. Or hog manure. Or anything other than glycerin. If we want to feed large quantities of glycerin to worms, we should compost it first. Worms need bacteria to function properly, and bacteria need the carbohydrates in carbon to thrive, but pure carbon glycerin would need to be massively cut with nitrogen in order to play.

Which takes us out of the worm business.

When my brother Jim was visiting over Christmas, he was jazzed by both the Plant, and the prospects for a worm business.

Unfortunately I have to tell him to forget it. We would have to ship worm food in daily. Shipping scraps to the worms is unsustainable.

Worms, like children, need consistency. And all we are going to have consistently at Piedmont Biofuels is glycerin.

Brian showed us some images of proper vermiculture operations, and none of them fit with our space. It was over for worms and us.

Despite our conclusion that Piedmont Biofuels would not be entering the worm business, Tes and I built a vermiculture digester in the back yard, just outside the Plant kitchen.

We dug out a shallow pit and lined it with hardware cloth to prevent predation from moles, which love to eat worms. We lined it with some cinder blocks we had lying around, and Tes pounded together a "way too heavy" lid made from an old garage door we retrieved from the woods behind the Moncure Museum of Art.

We filled the fortified pit with shredded paper, and some worms, and some food waste, and bingo, we were doing worm composting.

The trouble is we missed on the grade. We did nothing to provide drainage, and since the red clay of North Carolina tends to retain water, rather than let it percolate downward, we drowned our worms.

That felt like our first day of school. It meant tearing everything apart, backfilling with gravel, and adding a drain to our pit. Let's call it "Worm Tuition."

And back to vermiculture digestion we went. New worms. Newly drained system. Still a monster heavy top that took either a couple of people to lift, or one person with a good chiropractor.

That version worked for a while. We fed some kitchen food waste to the worms. Brian would come out to inspect, and encourage us, but we never harvested any castings to put into the world.

About the same time that Tes was leaving to chase after her elusive PhD, we needed some hourly help to clean up for our grand opening. We had been building a biodiesel plant for a year and a bit, and it felt like high time to cut a ribbon on something.

I needed some muscle, and so we hired Amanda, who was a freshly minted soil scientist from Minnesota. Her early job responsibilities included recycling, taking trash to the transfer station, and pretty much anything else that needed tending to. Including worms.

Brian convinced us that bringing food waste from seven blocks away would not cut too deeply into our goal of sustainability.

With his guidance, Amanda and I wrote and received a $7500 grant from DENR's "pollution prevention" division. The idea was that we would collect food waste that was headed for the landfill, and run it through a worm digester, and make valuable castings

*Amanda launched us into
the worm business.*

that we would take to market. We believed the energy we were wasting hauling food scraps around was offset by the landfill diversion we would be undertaking.

Our food waste was to come from Chatham Marketplace, and the idea was to sell castings back through the Marketplace. It was to be a wonderful "round trip loop" that would turn waste into money.

By the time we received our grant money, we were accomplished stewards of public funds. We were good at hitting milestones. We understood compliance. Public money is different from private money — and we get that.

We built a greenhouse, and a worm digester, and a "worm smoothie machine" to aid in the process. The worm smoothie machine was little more than a back yard chipper that Brian had lying around.

Screech modified Brian's chipper slightly. It was designed to take branches and spit out sawdust. We rigged it to take in zucchini rinds and spit out worm smoothies.

Worms are completely capable of digesting zucchini rinds without help. But when the rind is run through the worm smoothie machine, it acts as a "pre-digestion" step. Which means the worms can "eat more faster now." Which leads to more mating, and more cocoons, and a larger community that can take more food waste.

We might want to bear in mind that this is the master's perspective. It appears that when the human animal is involved, more of everything has no relationship to happiness. But despite our full knowledge of this, we tend to think that more pre-digested food is a good thing for a worm community.

When it came time to design our first digester I headed to NC State University with Brian to see the vermiculture operations they were operating. Their pre-digestion step was a five gallon plastic pail with a two-by-four for pulverization. And they had worm bins, with mechanical harvesting systems on the bottom.

I studied the harvesting system. It was a simple grate with a blade in a track that would move through the castings, breaking their surface tension, and allowing them to fall into a tray at the bottom of the system.

On our visit to NC State all the bins had electrically powered winches to move the bottom blades. I asked, on tour, if those could be hand cranked, and was told, "No, that would probably not work."

That didn't make sense to me. I thought about the sailboat and trailer in my woods. I used to sail it occasionally. A simple hand crank allowed me to move a huge weight out of the water onto dry land. I thought that a hand crank could surely provide the energy to harvest some worm poop.

We ignored the advice of the experts and built a stainless steel vermiculture digester with a hand crank on each end. Later I learned that hand cranks were commonplace in other systems, thereby depriving me of yet another patent, and forcing me to stay in the workforce rather that claiming my long overdue early retirement.

Just as we finished the fabrication of our first digester, Brian got the North Carolina legislature excited about vermiculture digestion for the food waste that comes out of their cafeteria. They bought our first unit from us.

We had a greenhouse, and a worm smoothie machine, and some money in hand, but we had sold our only worm bin.

So we built another one. This time we figured we would save some cash and built it out of galvanized steel. Galvanized is much cheaper than stainless. It's zinc, and does not rust. It's not something you want to weld on, but if you do have to weld on galvanized it helps to drink a lot of milk first. Drinking milk helps to keep you from vomiting when you are inhaling the poisonous fumes that zinc emits during the welding process.

But galvanized worm digester 1.1 was a big mistake. We filled it with shredded paper, and worms, and food waste, but the castings caused the galvanized steel to immediately rust. Castings are acidic.

It was a toxic reaction. Not good for the steel. Not good for the castings.

As a mid course correction, we riveted a plastic liner to the sides of the bin, and the plastic has worked great. As our worm education progressed, we learned that stainless gets high grades, galvanized flunks, and plastic is fine.

The whole trick is to have a way to harvest the castings from the bottom of the bin. Fill up a container with some bedding material, and some worms, and some food waste, and the castings will find their way to the bottom. They tend to knit themselves together in a unified layer with some help from a fungus that likes to tag along.

Harvesting from the bottom allows for minimal disruption of the worm community, rather than disrupting everything by going in through the top. Ours was more of a "continuous flow" design.

But when we brought our system online in a greenhouse, we cooked an entire batch of worms. We left them no place to get cool.

We invested in new worms, and improved the ventilation in the greenhouse, and we found ourselves wiped out by fire ants. Predation again.

Worms are livestock. They demand the same attention that any livestock demands. Keeping them safe, fed, and happily producing is the same task facing every livestock producer, from the cattle farmer to the beekeeper.

Our third sale for a vermiculture digester came from Larry's Beans. They are a coffee roaster in Raleigh that have become so obsessed with sustainability that selling coffee has become a sideline. Roasting and selling coffee is their core competency. But sustainability has lodged in their imagination. They have day-lit their facility, and they run a delivery bus on straight vegetable oil, and they make Piedmont Biofuels biodiesel available to the public in their front yard, and on and on. They are sustainability nut jobs, and their never ending quest for finding a different way of being led them to us.

Piedmont Biofuels suffers from youth. On the one hand youthful enthusiasm for societal change is our strong point. On the other it makes us envy high tech solutions that are beyond our reach.

We "engineer" a lot of products, but since we don't have a single engineer on staff we suffer from "engineering envy." Which means that when Larry's Beans wants to order a vermiculture digester, we need to run the design through 3D modeling software, fabricate everything to the highest possible quality, and spend a lot of time working on it.

For Larry's Beans that meant a Memo of Understanding, a down-payment, and a six-week lead time.

Our design-build crew are not big E.F. Schumacher readers. They are young, and brilliant, and creatures of the Net, and they do incredible things when it comes to moving liquids around. But they are not exactly students of "appropriate technology."

When I heard we were charging $4,000 for a simple vermiculture digester I intervened. I took our vast worm knowledge to Summer Shop at my house and set to work with my son Zafer, a Sawzall, and a 275 gallon "tote."

These are the containers I wrote about in the Piedmont Biofuels chapter that serve as an extraordinary part of our waste stream.

Our first attempt was a complete flop. We dismantled the tote, cut the wrong pattern out of both plastic and metal, and had to discard the entire effort. I shared my prototyping work with our design-build folks, and they took it from there. I wanted to enter the market with the $995 vermiculture digestion system, but the boys came up with a design that was almost double that. We started selling them only to find that the state felt a permit was required in order to operate one. So we applied for permits, and we found the state doesn't actually issue permits. They merely require them.

Thank you government. What we need is another pointless barrier to entry.

At about the time that I received the email from Bountiful Backyards, advertising their upcoming worm workshop, Piedmont Biofarm was in the midst of a severe cash crunch. A late pepper crop, combined with the brutal economic downturn left them unable to pay all of their workers. I looked around and spotted "money in the yard." Here we had a working vermiculture digester, and plastic garbage cans full of castings.

I played around with packaging for a couple of days, and settled on a plastic lined bag that was used by the folks who make Little Red Wagon Granola. They had an attractive display at Chatham Marketplace, and my children were eating their product, so I carefully removed their label from a spent pack, and filled it with worm castings. I borrowed the certified scale that Piedmont Biofarm takes to the farmers market, and found that exactly two pounds of castings made for a nicely plump bag.

I called Little Red Wagon to find out where to get bags, and brought in a sample order. It was the summer of 2009, and I had several children under foot. One day I took them to the plant and they spent the morning bagging worm castings. Filling each bag to exactly two pounds.

I then ran around town looking for worm castings for sale. Melinda at Country Home and Farm had bulk castings for sale for $1.00 a pound.

At a garden center in Carrboro, I found a five pound bag for five dollars, brought in from Florida. The garden center had previously brought in a load of bad worm castings — one that was full of pathogens — that spread plant disease to growers throughout the region. That experience left them wary of locally made castings.

Brian had told us about their castings distribution disaster, and as a result Amanda had set up a batch testing system with the North Carolina Department of Agriculture. She spent a dollar a pound on testing. My cursory market research indicated that we would have to have the highest price around.

When Amanda learned I was about to bring castings to market, she explained that we were not a "permitted facility" and that if we were to sell the worm castings as a fertilizer we would need to register and collect a fertilizer tax.

I can see that. Timothy McVeigh blew up the Murrow building in Oklahoma City with fertilizer. But worm castings would not have done the job. I believe in regulation. Except when they are silly and ridiculous.

The regulations stipulated that if we were a "soil amendment" no registration was required. I felt that we should use the label to get our message out. Sort of like Dr. Bronner's soap, only without the insanity.

Tami and I then went to work on labeling. I picked Amanda's brain for some details about the product, and I wrote a Casting FAQ's, which we printed as a sticker for the back of the bag.

It's prefaced with the image of a worm wondering, "If I were a fertilizer…"

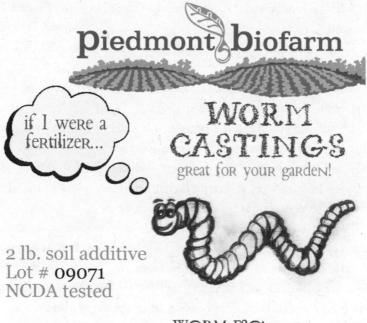

piedmont biofarm

if I were a fertilizer…

WORM CASTINGS
great for your garden!

2 lb. soil additive
Lot # 09071
NCDA tested

WORM FaQ's

What's a worm casting? It's worm poop.

Why would I want to buy worm poop? It's a great soil amendment for bedding plants, houseplants, and gardens.

So it's like fertilizer? Yup. And just like fertilizer you can think of it in ratios. Pick up a bag of fertilizer sometime and you will see an NPK listing. The N is for nitrogen. The P is for phosphorus. The K is for potassium. Worm castings have an average NPK ratio of 1.6-0.25-1.

Is it organic? Yup. Worms concentrate organic matter, so their castings break down much faster than food scraps in a compost pile. Organic matter also has a C:N ratio. That's a measure of how much carbon and nitrogen are present. There's always more carbon than nitrogen. Worm castings tend to average 12.5 :1.

What's the PH? Worm castings average around 6.77.
Is it safe? We don't suggest eating it. But it is great to add to your soil. It has trace minerals in it, and we get every batch tested by the North Carolina Department of Agriculture before we take it to market. That way we know it is free of pathogens that can harm your bedding plants.

Where do they come from? Piedmont Biofarm, on the eastern edge of Pittsboro. We collect food waste (some from Chatham Marketplace), and run it through our vermiculture digestion system. More info on Piedmont Biofarm: www.biofuels.coop/food/biofarm

If you would like to buy in bulk, call Amanda at 919-321-8260. We don't make a lot of these- the worms are virtually hand raised, so make sure you call ahead.

Why so expensive? We are the only permitted vermiculture facility powered by human food waste in North Carolina. If you would like to save money on your castings, check out Country Home and Farm on Small St. in Pittsboro. Over there Melinda sells cheaper castings in bulk that come from hog waste.

Can I just get my own worms and make my own for free? Yup. Please do. You can take Worm Workshops at the Abundance Foundation next to Piedmont Biofarm, or you can go to Bountiful Backyards in Durham.
Why would we advertise for the competition? Because we think the world needs to change. One way to start to change is by making dirt. Soil can be a renewable resource if it is treated right. And worm castings—from anyone—can be an excellent start.

We labeled the carefully filled bags, and we were on the shelf at Chatham Marketplace the next day. I sold the castings to them for $2.50 a pound, and they sold them to their customers for $3.50 a pound.

I was uncertain how we would make out with our $7.00 bags of castings for sale.

They sold out in three days. Amanda restocked them, and we have been selling castings ever since.

I knew we could fetch a premium for being locally produced. Our community gets that. They are glad we are producing, and they pay a premium for our products — from garlic to fuel to bug spray — because they understand that for an economy to function properly somebody has to "make" something.

Part of our community is vehemently opposed to confined animal feeding operations (CAFOs), and many of them welcomed worm castings that did not come from hog waste. In the past Piedmont Biofuels has been bruised for making biodiesel out of waste poultry fat. We took a beating from the vegans and the anti-CAFO crowd.

I didn't have the heart to explain that in order to create the castings we are running a worm CAFO.

We now sell castings in bulk, directly to growers, and bagged product to Chatham Marketplace, and to the Abundance Foundation, which also sells books about vermiculture, and glycerin soap, and other stuff to those who tour our eco-industrial park.

As our worm business started contributing to the revenues of both Piedmont Biofarm, and to design-build — the guys building the digesters — we connected with Ben from Carolina Worm Castings.

Ben had an entirely different business model over in Apex, North Carolina. While we used red wigglers, a variety of worm that stays near the surface, he was using African night crawlers, which would readily escape from our digesters. While we were feeding food waste to our worms, under a permitted process and testing for soil borne diseases, he was buying compost for his worms. No permits or testing required.

The good thing about Ben is that he was focused exclusively on worms. He was selling castings through a series of "batch digesters," and was running out of space at his home in Apex.

Ben and I spent a few days walking around the park discussing our various approaches and belief systems and concluded that a merger was in order. Not a merger of worms, but a merger of companies. Piedmont Biofarm agreed to sell all of its worm assets — its plastic lined digester with worms, its worm smoothie machine, the screening mechanism that Screech had built, and all of its bags and scales and anything else associated with the business to Carolina Worm Castings.

Ben agreed to rent the hallway of Building 3 so that he could have some heated space in which to expand. He also agreed to hire Ana Marie, who had been maintaining our worm operations. Piedmont Biofuels agreed to make the space available, and the Abundance Foundation agreed to let Carolina Worm Castings take over the worm workshops.

It was a meeting of minds that put us squarely in the worm business. It could be seen as just another tenant moving to the park, or as just another startup, or as a potentially decent living for two, or it can be seen the way I like to think of it, as the confluence of tuition, experience, and dedication which will no doubt succeed.

Piedmont Biofarm

SELLING WORM CASTINGS didn't save the farm. All it did was demonstrate that the farm had "money in the yard." It had an asset in its digester, and product lying around, and when worm castings went to market and were converted into cash, other things followed suit.

Garlic, mostly.

Doug Jones, who is a genius propagator of vegetables, runs Piedmont Biofarm. His passion is for seed saving, variety trials, and the improvement of different genetic lines.

But that doesn't pay the rent. Most of that sort of work is done at universities, where funding streams exist for research. And Doug didn't start with a bunch of money. It is not an exaggeration to say Doug has cobbled together an impressive farming operation from scraps he found lying around.

Back to garlic. Over the years he has developed his own line of bioregionally selected garlic. That is, his garlic performs well in our soils, with our pests, amongst our plant diseases. And because it has been "developed" for that, it is easy to sell as seed to other garlic producers in the region.

Garlic goes into the ground in the fall, and is harvested in the spring. One of the challenges for the seed producer is how to store that crop through a brutally hot and humid North Carolina summer. Especially when you lack the capital to build proper storage.

One year Doug tried to use part of his greenhouse. Not so good. The next year he gained access to an abandoned building over in Oilseed Community, got the electricity turned on, and outfitted its basement with a dehumidifier. Better, still not the best storage results in the world. Anything stored in a North Carolina summer without air conditioning tends to mildew, and mildewing garlic means yield loss.

And about the time that worm castings came on the market, Doug started selling seed garlic in bulk, in advance of the season. Just because it gets planted in the fall, doesn't mean it can't be sold sooner — especially to growers with better storage assets. In an extremely tight time for Piedmont Biofarm, Doug got the money out of storage and into payroll.

I am not entirely accurate when I say that Doug's seed development work doesn't pay the rent. Garlic eaters in our town can go to our Piggly Wiggly and get garlic from China for $3 a pound. Those who prefer their eating to have a sustainability bent can go

Doug Jones is a pillar of the local sustainable farming community.

to Chatham Marketplace and get locally produced product for $5 a pound. Selling garlic as seed, Doug fetches $9 a pound. His years of persistently sticking with garlic seed selection do add a value that comes back to his operation.

I have to say that Doug is a complicated man, and that it has taken me years to understand his genius. I once traveled to Pennsylvania to give a talk to the Eat Fresh, Eat Local movement at Dickinson College. I titled the speech "Foot Caught in the Food Shed Door." Here is what I said:

Blog

I have a deep love for Meredith Wilson's *The Music Man.* Largely because it is about a traveling salesman, which, at the end of the day is what I am.

For those not familiar with that play, the poor fellow falls in love with a local girl and decides to stick around. He calls it "getting his foot caught in the door," which is a term I often use when describing my wife, Tami.

Saving seeds is one of Doug Jones' major passions.

But the idea of getting my foot caught in the door and sticking around also applies to my relationship to our local food shed.

I'm going to start with sweet potatoes. Doug Jones is a master agricultural genius that moved to an intentional community in our North Carolina county years ago and produced in a single season more sweet potatoes than anyone could eat.

I laughed. Nutcase. I had eaten sweet potatoes at Tami's grandmother's house. They were in a casserole topped with marshmallows and they were downright nasty. Of course no one would want to eat them.

Doug abandoned his work at his cohousing community farm and plugged into Central Carolina Community College where he was instrumental in propagating a "land lab," at the sustainable agriculture program, and a college-based CSA.

At the time I didn't know what local food was. Much less cared. I did value the program at the college. I could see how having a unique sustainable agriculture program was good for our economy and our community. I'm a business guy. I like to see people moving product, and I was pleased to see Doug moving students.

I was teaching a renewable energy class at the college, so I was allowed to participate in his CSA. I started picking up food in boxes. It was annoying. It often meant an extra trip to the college, and at the time I was running around on precious homemade fuel. But I wanted to support the venture.

I'm not sure my family ate much of the food out of most of those early boxes. I think a high percentage went to compost, because we didn't really change our eating habits. We simply added a new box of weirdo food.

When Doug became restless at the community college we decided it might be a good idea for him to set up a commercial farming operation in the front lawn of our biodiesel operation. And he did that. He transformed a vacant lot into a fecund and remarkable growing operation.

That's when I learned that the sweet potato should be a staple in the North Carolinian diet. That's when I started cooking them six ways from Sunday and started using them as food. Tami and I have two teenage boys under foot, and I often turn the kitchen into "Estill Family Food Labs" where I do science experiments on actual human subjects, and in doing so we have learned how to eat out of our CSA box, and we have come to celebrate the work of Doug Jones.

I'm guessing that it is coincidental, but I have noticed the rise in sweet potato recipes since Doug has come to town. You can now order everything from sweet potato fries to sweet potato ice cream at area restaurants.

❀ ❀ ❀

I was on Topsail Island, on the coast of North Carolina when I read Michael Pollan's *Omnivore's Dilemma*. As it did for so many others, the book had a profound impact on me.

I had heard of a fellow in Michigan who wanted to move to North Carolina to farm. I knew that Doug needed help getting his operation to expand and so I began pacing on the back deck of our rented beach house and making cell calls.

In order to land the fellow from Michigan he would need some equity. At the time Piedmont Biofarm was not incorporated. So I got a hold of Kathie, who created a corporation.

We arranged for Doug to take control of the shares, which I owned, and with the promise of equity lined up, I landed the farmer from Michigan.

That didn't work out so well. He was more like me. Sort of a "gardener" type. The business of sustainable farming in North Carolina is grueling work. It requires diligence from sunup to sundown, through the extreme heat, seven days a week.

It's back-breaking, and hot, and edifying, and marginally profitable.

Piedmont Biofarm, the corporation, was born, but it wasn't long before it was just Doug and his crew, and since there didn't seem any need for equity to attract partners, the corporate side went dormant. In the meantime, Doug plugged away at converting the land around our chemical plant into a fecund masterpiece.

There are two ways to view Doug's farm. The first is to see it as a money making venture that is exploding with produce and seed varieties and tours and eaters. The second is to recognize it as something on a vacant lot next door.

We weren't doing anything with the land. Nor did we need it for anything. And Doug moved in. His tractor implements, and indeed his pepper beds, run right up to the spill-containment walls of our tank farm.

From Piedmont Biofuel's perspective Doug's farm is a marginal contributor. From a financial perspective it can easily be viewed as a "phantom load." The farm will take space, and fuel, and electricity, and bookkeeping, and water, and as its profits have grown it has gradually begun to pay for all of these things.

Before long, the Abundance Foundation took an interest in the seed saving that Doug was doing. My wife, Tami, runs Abundance and she has a small office on our project. Abundance has devoted its efforts to local food and renewable energy and community development, and at one point they decided to focus on Piedmont Biofarm.

That presented a problem, as there is a firewall between Tami and myself. Money that is donated to Abundance cannot benefit either of us personally. And I owned 100% of Piedmont Biofarm.

So I gave all of the shares to Doug.

With no ownership stake, Tami was free to raise money for Doug's endeavors.

Doug has gone on to launch a variety of Asian collard seeds into the Fedco catalog, and has also been picked up by Seeds of Change. As a breeder of plants it is an honor for your selections to make the seed catalogs. On those dark winter nights, when gardeners everywhere are reading the catalogs, planning their gardens and dreaming of spring, it is comforting to know that Doug's variety selections are in play.

Being surrounded by Piedmont Biofarm contributes mightily to the overall strength of our enterprise. Almost everyone on project values local food. Many of us consume the food of Piedmont Biofarm. And it is somehow spiritually important to come to work in the morning and be surrounded by fields of okra and garlic and peppers and greens of all sorts.

Our obsession with local food goes even deeper than that. We once had a group of students visit from Davidson College. They camped in the back yard, used our locker rooms for showers, and used the kitchen for shared meals. They were hard-working volunteers.

I remember how jarring it was to see their box of Lucky Charms in our kitchen. They dined on Sunbeam bread, and a variety of highly refined non-food products, and I think that everyone on project was somewhat stunned.

Those of us who have immersed ourselves in the local food shed, whether sticking to a hundred mile diet or not, have become so accustomed to large quantities of exquisite food that it tends to be the thing we miss the most when we are forced to be "off project."

Ours is a place where local food and local fuel collide, which means that many of the people around our place are "foodies," and as such, we place an incredibly high value on the existence of Piedmont Biofarm. We like being surrounded by local food production.

Were we to keep a ledger on Piedmont Biofarm we would find its financial contribution marginal, and its spiritual contribution exceptional. Pick a yardstick.

By most accounts Doug is an agricultural giant. He was named "Farmer of the Year" in 2010 by the Carolina Farm Stewardship

Association. Check. He is exceptionally hard-working. Check. But I will say that incorporating seed saving with production agriculture is nigh on impossible. Especially when it also involves a near-constant turnover of willing, eager young interns.

What you want to be able to tell your new intern is, "Here is how you pick, now go and pick that row."

That could lead to lots of satisfaction for both entities in the transaction. Doug would get the row picked, and the intern would get the benefit of meaningful employment, as in "I picked that row."

But because there is seed saving involved, Doug wants the row picked to the seventh plant on the left, then three plants skipped, then picked to the fence line, then skipping the fourth plant from the middle and so on. It's a recipe for failure. Doug is sure to get his prize specimens accidentally harvested, and the picker is sure to feel like they have done a bad thing for the farm.

It's complicated. Doug's complicated. Farming is complicated. Interns are complicated.

I like to skip the complicated parts. Despite the frustrations that arise with the property, most of us savor its leeks, long for its peppers, and adore its rolling fields of scenic food which surround us and greet us when we arrive at the plant gate each morning.

State of the Bubble

O NE OF THE DRIVERS on our project is Bob Armantrout. He
had an interesting career in biodiesel prior to moving in to
our project. By the time he arrived at Oilseed Community he had
worked for Pacific Biodiesel in Hawaii — one of the true pioneers
of the American biodiesel industry — and he had worked for
Biodiesel Industries.

Bob is an "operations" guy. He likes to plan, budget, hit tar-
gets, make forecasts and operate businesses that are financially
sustainable. He holds a Masters in Business Administration, and
he is a little older than most of the people on project.

For me he is a breath of fresh air.

Occasionally my scattered, feckless ways drive him nuts, but
somehow he has managed to check his rage and fit in beautifully.
As an operations guy, Bob is always hungry for information.

On one occasion he pulled me aside and suggested that we
do a "State of the Bubble" address on the last Friday of each
month, where we could update everyone on the month that had
passed.

It was to be a business meeting. Design-Build could give their
update on projects that had shipped versus what remained on the
backlog, Research and Analytics could explain their progress, or

lack thereof, Production could talk about the gallons of biodiesel for the month, and so on.

And perhaps more importantly, other businesses on project could weigh in. We could learn how the farm was doing. Whether they needed more eaters. Or had a surplus of this or that. The idea was that each business would get two minutes to present their status to the group.

On the first Bubble meeting Bob ran the stopwatch. And we gave it an earnest try. The kitchen was filled with people. The meeting was succinct and crisp. And it flowed into a social evening — the beer started flowing, and it was perceived to be a smashing success by all.

We planned to do it regularly, and everyone would get a chance to give an update "from his or her corner of the bubble." On our project we love orbs with corners.

At the time Bob used to be interested in "org charts." Tami found some clear plastic beach balls, and I blew one of them up, and drew an impossible org chart on it to make Bob happy. It had dotted lines, and solid lines, and listed all sorts of businesses and organizations on it. It was in the spirit of Laurence Sterne's plot lines. In the *Life and Opinions of Tristram Shandy, Gentleman,* which some literary historians like to place as the "first novel," he does some impossible diagrammatic work in an effort to reveal to his "gentle readers" which direction the plot is headed. It's hysterical. My "bubble chart" was inspired by Sterne.

It didn't take long for the Bubble meeting to shift. With the addition of the beach ball prop came the passing of the beach ball, which made it more like a talking stick process than a meeting governed by a stopwatch. At the heart of the notion of the "talking stick" is the idea that whoever holds the stick holds the floor, and everyone else just listens. It is supposed to be an equalizer. That way meetings aren't dominated by the loudest, or the most articulate. It lets the quiet people be heard.

And the passing of the bubble changed the dynamic of the meeting.

One thing that happened almost immediately is that the talk shifted from business to personal. People quit drinking and doing drugs and started talking about it with the group. We would take the beach ball and talk about it, and suddenly whatever we might have been doing in our working lives seemed much less important.

Jaime would come from a weekend away, hug the beach ball to her chest, and weep about her joy to be home. She would enumerate the absences she felt, from local food to people who loved her. And when she would do that, suddenly none of us cared about the strength of the Abundance Foundation's balance sheet.

Soon the State of the Bubble became where people would go to announce their engagements and their pregnancies. Simon jumped into the creek behind Oilseed Community and panned up some gold to make a wedding ring for Jessica. He brought

Bob Armantrout holds the beach ball at a "state of the bubble" meeting.

the vial of ore to a State of the Bubble to break the news of their engagement to the group.

Another event that had a significant impact on our State of the Bubble meeting was the explosion we had in our tank farm.

Our tank farm is like a giant above-ground concrete swimming pool filled with ten thousand-gallon tanks that stand four stories high and are plumbed with pumps and manifolds and pipes every which way. Eighteen-wheelers full of liquids pull up and drop their loads. Or they pull up and we load them with product. And they drive away.

Our plant has been under construction since it opened. We do "hot work" everywhere. We weld. We cut. We use high voltages. And we do so amidst explosive materials. Our fabrication crew is expert at how to build a chemical plant while we are moving big, dangerous liquids around. We understand the creation of negative pressure, and the purging of flammable material from lines, and we have been working in it for years.

I was walking up the stairs to the control room when I heard the giant hissing boom that immediately made me turn and run toward the tank farm.

When I arrived on the other side of Building 3, I saw Ponytail stripping off his burning pants, with the bare, burnt skin of his back exposed.

Others were gathered around in horror. Rick was lying on the concrete floor of the tank farm twitching. His eyes had rolled into the back of his head. I jumped the wall and took up my position at his head, taking it into my lap. PJ was on first aid. Rick's leg was crushed and lying at a funny angle.

I was a lifeguard as a kid, which means I had some first aid training. And I had pulled some kids out of swimming pools. I had done some CPR on dummies.

But when Rick's head was in my hands, the only thing I could think about was the death of my brother Mark several months earlier. I was holding Mark's hand when he died. And I had spent months trying to talk him out of doing that. I helped load Mark into the ambulance at the hospital and I held his hand as we made the trip to his living room. I dabbed a washcloth on his sweating forehead and I said little things like, "It's not dying time, big'uy. We are going to make it home OK."

And we did, in the early afternoon. He listened. And he complied. And by dinnertime that night Mark was gone.

Holding Rick I began the same platitudes, as if they were tapes inside of me and I simply hit "Play." Rick is an industrial welder. And beekeeper. He is strong as an ox and as tough as nails. I ran my hand through his hair and explained that he was going to be OK, and that an ambulance was on the way, and that he just needed to hang in there, and that he was going to make it.

Unlike my brother Mark, Rick came back to life in my arms. His eyes came back into their sockets. He recognized me. I asked him his name and he knew who he was.

Shortly after he reached clarity the paramedics arrived and I was shooed away from the scene. Which was good. Not only was I underqualified for that job, but also someone needed to call Tracy, his wife. And I did that next.

Several days after the accident we had a State of the Bubble meeting. One of our people, Ponytail, was in the burn unit at UNC Hospital, and Rick was a few floors away in intensive care. Our project was scared sick.

Everyone that night was fixated on safety and permitting. Everyone was looking for a place to lay blame. Everyone was terrified that either Rick or Ponytail would die and that it would be over for us.

Those of us in the biodiesel industry remembered when a man died in South Carolina while grinding inside a tank used for glycerin storage. The industry took a black eye. On the forums I characterized it as a welding accident, and I shrugged it off. One of the questions I left on Infopop was "I wonder if anyone ever died trying to produce petroleum for our vehicles."

When West Central Soy had a similar accident, they spun off Renewable Energy Group in order to get some distance on plant fabrication liability. When Tommy Evan's tank blew up in Wilson, he shut his biodiesel plant down. Years later Imperium in Gray's Harbor would do the same thing.

We understood that we were on the doorstep of a "plant closing event," and those at the State of the Bubble were scared and nervous and searching.

The night of the accident, after all the ambulances had left and after our guys were safely tucked into the hands of UNC Hospital, I headed to the Chatham Marketplace, as I often do at quitting time. Mary the manager was enjoying a cigarette on a milk crate out back. We are friends. Our spirits often lift at the mere sight of one another. On that occasion when she asked me how it was going, I collapsed into a complete break down in her arms.

At that moment I felt we were ruined.

But it turned out not to be the case. Ponytail checked into the burn unit and was completely restored to health. He still shows up around hunting season to shoot deer about the place.

And Rick made an amazing recovery.

I was still in shock from the accident, and I went to our mayor's house to discuss it. I am an ally of his, and he is an ally of mine. He was unfazed. His brother-in-law Kevin was also there, and he too was nonchalant about it. They explained that it was merely an industrial accident, and not ruination. And that industrial accidents happen all the time.

I was both surprised and comforted by their responses to our accident, and I was delighted that its news never found its way into the local media. "Accident at Piedmont" never became a story we had to confront.

Our local fire marshal was also supportive. In his line of work he is accustomed to much worse. He shows up at the house on fire, finds the dead mother and child, and meets the school bus with the news. Then he calls the father at work.

He felt the event could trigger a new level of compliance for the plant, which was with the Occupational Safety and Health Administration. That didn't happen, but we went ahead and undertook OSHA compliance anyway.

We formed a safety committee, and started a long journey of safety meetings, video screenings, checklists, and standard operating procedures.

Over time, safety has faded from the Bubble meetings. That is more of a Piedmont thing and has a slot at each one of our weekly staff meetings.

When people gather in the plant kitchen, to toss the beach ball around, they tend to be tenants of the park, or residents of Oilseed, or farmers from about the place, many of which are oblivious to our accident, or to how it fundamentally shifted Piedmont's culture.

The bubble is much larger than Piedmont at this point, as is the whole project. And the State of the Bubble meeting lives on.

It's funny. The State of the Bubble meeting is merely a huge chunk of "process," and we are not really "process" people. In *Small is Possible* I described a series of lifeboats in our area. Blue Heron Farm, a neighboring cohousing community has invested heavily in process, and I have to say that our State of the Bubble meeting has taken a page from their songbook.

It certainly was not what Bob intended. But it works. And we are grateful for it.

Fighting Town Hall

ONE OF THE PROBLEMS with new industrial development is that the regulatory community, and often the political community, is comfortable with the way things are. Which means new ideas don't always fit in so well, and are not always welcomed.

One of the things we have accidentally developed over the years at Piedmont Biofuels is an active consulting business. Clients from across the United States, and Canada, and even Latin America, have hired us to consult on their biodiesel projects. And one of the first things we counsel, when it comes to regulation, is to have the code references ready to cite prior to meeting with regulators.

Regulators prefer that. They tend to be in way over their heads, often strapped by a public that refuses to raise taxes to fund their endeavors, and as a result they tend to be spread thin. By arriving at the fire marshal's door with citations in hand, the permitting process tends to be much smoother.

That is, do not show up without a clue to announce you are building a biodiesel plant. The minute they grab their codebook, and look up "f" for "fuel," you are doomed to a protracted swim through the permitting process that will include a significant amount of backstroke.

We sell a booklet entitled "Gospel Permits" to our consulting customers.

Piedmont hasn't suffered from that. Our relationship with the fire marshal has been excellent. There has been significant back and forth and both of us have learned a terrific amount.

But we haven't been as lucky with the folks who handle our wastewater.

Pittsboro, North Carolina has always been a poorly run southern town. That's one of the reasons it has remained small. Its covenant is simple: don't tax the citizens, and provide a minimum of services. That will control growth, and keep everything pretty much the way it has always been. Which is the way many of our politicians like it.

In the case of wastewater, that means that Pittsboro is running a 1950s vintage treatment plant that actually loses capacity every time the regulations are improved. That is, when the Department of Environment and Natural Resources decreases the amount of nitrates that can be released into the watershed, Pittsboro can only comply by decreasing its discharges. When the Environmental Protection Agency decides that Robeson Creek is 100% degraded and no longer able to accept effluent from the Town of Pittsboro, it means the town ends up getting fined pretty much every time there is a big rain event.

One of the results of Pittsboro's chronic mismanagement of its wastewater treatment facility is that new industry does not come to town. Combine that with apparent incompetence by town employees, and you have a recipe for the failure of new industrial endeavors.

When we bought our sewer allocation from the Town of Pittsboro, we were required to file an "Industrial Waste Survey" form, which we did. We calculated the peak amount of discharge for our newly built chemical plant, and we spelled out what we intended to do.

They cashed our check and everyone was happy. For about six months.

Around that time we had worked the bugs out of our process and were ready to take our plant out for a spin. We spent the first six months making ten thousand gallons of fuel here, and fifteen thousand gallons of fuel there, and our wastewater discharges corresponded accordingly.

In spring of 2007, I went to the Town's public works manager and asked how we were doing. I told him we were discharging at the right time of day, as we had been told to do, and that we were finally ready to crank our production.

I was told, "We don't even notice you, Lyle."

Which made me feel confident. I went back to the plant, told our production and management team we were good on the wastewater front, and we pushed the throttle down. We made 40K gallons of fuel that month, and to do so we released 40K gallons of wastewater.

At which point the Town called to say we had destroyed their wastewater treatment plant.

It turns out that the public works manager had not been talking to the fellow who operated the wastewater treatment plant. He was slowly being poisoned by our releases. He was busy doing trace routes of the sewer system to find out where that yellow liquid was coming from, and eventually he tracked it back to us.

The day the treatment plant went down (all of the microbes in its anaerobic digestion system had been killed by our biodiesel wash water), I got the call and headed for their facility. To me it did not appear to be a mystery. It looked like our discharge.

They were stunned. When I suggested it was exactly what we had filed in our industrial waste survey they scratched their heads and went looking for their copy. "Maybe Alice has it over at Town Hall," one of them said.

She didn't. Public works didn't have a copy. And the guys doing the work at the wastewater plant were oblivious. It was as if they didn't even know there was a biodiesel plant on the edge of town. We provided them a copy of the one we had filed, since they had lost ours.

At which point the State proceeded to fine the Town, and the Town proceeded to fine us $20,000.

Wow. To put this into context, another biodiesel producer in Missouri ran into regulatory trouble at about the same time. What they did was load a tanker truck with crude biodiesel glycerin bottoms — which is far more toxic than our biodiesel wash water — and they slipped out in the night and knowingly discharged it into a living creek. They received a $10,000 fine and a suspended sentence.

We were trying to play by the rules, but an incompetent bureaucracy was against us.

When the news broke, Piedmont went from being a model for environmental stewardship to "mister big polluter," and it was the first time our brand took a body blow in the community. No one cared about the facts. All that mattered was that we had been fined.

We paid our fine, with the understanding that once it was paid we would be able to use the Town's sewer system again. That didn't happen. Once our fine was paid, they still couldn't take our discharge.

By the time the Town had forgotten about us, a developer rolled in, bought all of the land around us, and filed to have it rezoned. We are on land that is zoned "industrial," and the developer wanted the land on all sides to become commercial/residential. His vision was to build the region's largest shopping mall, complete with condominiums where happy shoppers might want to live.

I fought against the project. It made no sense to me for our town to take its last bit of industrially zoned land and convert it into a shopping mall. For me it meant a space that was destined to make "things" was being converted to a space that was destined to make "change," and I thought it was a foolhardy move for our community.

There were protests, and rallies, and I did what I could, but I lost that one. Our Town Fathers thought it best if a big mall could come to town.

The mall never got built. The "downturn" of 2009 came along, and when many area developments failed, it turned out there were not enough consumers to support the beast, so it remains covered in cut-over pine trees to this day. Even the surveyor's stakes are starting to rot and fade.

But that is just lucky for us. It doesn't change the notion that in America today the mindset of our ruling class leans toward consumption rather than production. Why not turn your last piece of industrial land into a place where people can buy more stuff from China they don't need?

❋ ❋ ❋

My most bruising match with the Town of Pittsboro came with the municipal election of 2007. A group called Pittsboro Together had fielded a wonderful group of candidates who I supported. The project is in Pittsboro, but I don't live in Pittsboro. In Pittsboro, elections are won and lost by two votes.

Since most of Tami's and my net worth is inside the town limits of Pittsboro, (the fence at Piedmont Biofuels is the dividing line), we thought we should vote in the upcoming election. But we had a problem. Since the plant is zoned "industrial," no one can live there. Which means we needed a place to live in town.

So we leased a room in a big house on West Street. We figured that if we had a place to legally live, and a significant investment in the town, no one would mind if we cast our ballots there.

That was not one of our better ideas.

A reporter from the *Chapel Hill News* caught wind of our idea and emerged as a muckraker journalist wannabe. Unlike the real thing, however, this one repeatedly got the story wrong.

Our attempt to register to vote in town was turned down by the Board of Elections. They were kind about it, and said that thousands of people every year make the same mistake, and that if your residence in town is not your primary residence it is not allowed. People with houses at the beach routinely try to register in the community where they have investments, and are told it doesn't work that way. Our mistake was routine and commonplace.

But the *Chapel Hill News* was hungry for eyeballs, and Tami and I are just public figures enough to garner some readership, so they impaled us with inaccurate reporting.

The reporter asked, "Who owns the house you leased?"

I honestly replied, "I don't know. I think it is some builder in Apex."

She found out the house had been subleased by Randy Voller, Pittsboro's mayor, and thought she had caught me in a lie. They went to press with charges of "election fraud."

At the time I was a columnist for the *Chapel Hill News*, and when the story broke that I was up on charges of election fraud I was sacked. I tried to explain that their coverage was wrong, but they didn't listen to me and they whipped it into the headlines.

Tami and I were skewered in the press. I started running some backchannel coverage via email to Mark Schultz, the editor of the paper. Most of my subject lines read, "Wrong Again."

The reality was there was no charge of election fraud. There was no investigation. There was nothing more than an honest mistake, an incompetent reporter, and a lot of headlines. It even turned out that the house we had leased was owned by a builder in Apex.

Facts didn't matter.

Detractors of Lyle and Tami, and detractors of Piedmont Biofuels, had a field day. And it was a rotten time of life. Suddenly it appeared that the "big polluters" had got their comeuppance after all, and our little polarized community seemed delighted to eat a couple of their own.

Once the dust had settled, Mark Schultz ran a short retraction that no one noticed, and re-hired me as a columnist. Nothing changed except our reputation, which to this day has been tarnished by the event.

In 2008, Mayor Voller won again, as did Pamela Baldwin, and in 2009, Michael Fiocco was elected to the board, giving us two progressive votes. In 2010 we will win our third vote and we will at long last be able to govern our town with a progressive slate of politicians.

It is hard to imagine what that might look like. We could be the first carbon-free community in the Southeast. And we could cooperate with the county board for the first time in a generation. We could work together, rather than sitting around casting aspersions on ideas for a clean renewable future. We could tax carbon, and use the money to buy a filing cabinet to store industrial wastewater surveys. We could transform ourselves from a poorly run southern town into a model of stewardship for the future.

And at that point, companies like Piedmont Biofuels could give up fighting town hall.

The Abundance Foundation

N<small>O ONE IS ENTIRELY CLEAR</small> where the idea for the Abundance Foundation originated. I believe it was launched at our kitchen table, but Rachel swears it happened in the hot tub. I tend to have a policy of agreeing with Rachel, so I am not going to fight it.

When we started our backyard biodiesel project, Rachel worked full time as an automotive instructor at Central Carolina Community College. We taught a "biofuels" class as part of the continuing education program, and I taught an "energy" class, which is where Energy Blog originated. And at the College we created a "foundation account," to which people could make tax-deductible donations to our endeavors.

It was our charity. In the early days, my brother Mark was one of the large contributors. He didn't quite understand what we were messing around with in biodiesel, but he understood that we needed some cash, and so he donated. I had forgotten about that, until the State Energy Conference in 2009, where Mark was awarded a posthumous plaque for his efforts in renewable energy, and they somehow knew about his donations.

With the charitable part taken care of by the college, we formed our first corporation, Piedmont Biofuels Cooperative as a "C" corporation. It was a cooperative, but it was not a charity, and it was allowed to make a profit. Later we formed Piedmont Biofuels Industrial as a Limited Liability Corporation (LLC), also created as a money-making venture.

Rachel left the college and joined us at Industrial, and shortly thereafter the rate at which the college foundation performed became painstakingly slow. When we needed money to attend a conference, we would put in our request, and the college would need to think about it until past the conference registration date.

Donations, it seemed, vanished into the great wall of state-operated bureaucratic machinery, and we became disillusioned with the performance of the foundation we had created.

We felt we needed to be fleeter of foot. If I recall correctly it was about the same time that our Coop moved from having just me and Leif and Rachel to having an actual board of directors, and in doing so we ground our own performance to a halt.

When it was just Rachel, Leif, and me things happened at the speed of sound. Once we put a volunteer board in place, our high performance ended. I recall one conversation in which board

My brother Mark Estill was an early financial contributor to Central Carolina Community College and went on to lead the financial aspects of Piedmont Biofuels.

members argued for several months on whether we should insulate our south-facing passive solar "grease-warming zone." What we could have built in a week took months of discussion before it could be completed.

So with the College foundation moving like molasses in January, and a Coop mired in group decision making, Rachel and I were frustrated. So we joined in with Tami and formed our own nonprofit corporation.

As was our preference, we did it quickly. Kathie Russell helped us with the legal paperwork, and we applied for non-profit status with the IRS with a mission statement that said we were dedicated to "renewable energy, local food, and community," and we were on our way. We rounded up donations, and put solar thermal panels on the Moncure School when we learned they had no hot water for kids to wash their hands.

And we took donations for the Coop. People threw in old trucks, and small amounts of cash, and Abundance became a crutch that helped hold our ailing biodiesel cooperative together. Abundance bought us a property with a double-wide on it for use as intern housing.

Suddenly we had a charity again. Tami was in charge, and projects flew out the door. Decisions were rapid, made with a single phone call, meetings were over dinner, and the Abundance Foundation went from zero to having impact in no time at all. Andrea Young jumped in as a volunteer and began "friend raising" in earnest.

The name, Abundance, of course, was inspired by the teachings of John Breckenridge, a brilliant therapist in Silk Hope. One of the messages that John perpetually puts out is that we do not have to live in a world of scarcity, but rather, can choose a world of abundance.

John promotes the concept of the cosmic waiter, who is standing patiently at all of our tables, waiting to take our order. Many people sit at the table and dally.

John Breckenridge has provided our project with wise counsel and sage advice along the way.

"I want to order the lobster, but lobster is too rich for my diet."

"Um. I'm not sure what I want."

"I would really like the lobster, but I'm afraid I can't afford it."

"Maybe I should hold off."

"The lobster looks wonderful, but I'm not sure we are allowed to eat crustaceans from the sea floor anymore."

So while some people ponder their order, others get everything they want. Which is why the tagline of the Abundance Foundation is "Getting Everything You Want or Something Better..."

Abundance is clearly something John manifested. We just did the work. And the trajectory of Abundance was the same as the Coop. It grew to a certain point that it needed a "proper" board of directors, for which Tami and I selected an elite crew. Once there was a real board, work slowed down and instead of getting things done in the world, Abundance started professionalizing its operations.

Tami hired on as the executive director. Rachel became the board president. I was thrown off the board in order to eliminate any conflict of interest. And a firewall was erected so that the

Abundance board meetings are typically fun social events.

work of the Abundance Foundation could not benefit Piedmont Biofuels Industrial, or the eco-industrial park.

At which point Abundance was off and running. It helped the Town of Pittsboro amp up its Christmas parade, and it threw a marvelous Mardi Gras party, and it took over plant tours and took over the sale of tchotchke — t-shirts and soaps and jigsaw puzzles and the like.

Abundance raised money for seed-saving projects, and took in donations from private individuals and family foundations, and it became the "fiscal sponsor" of a variety of groups who had not established their legal nonprofit status. For example, they became the fiscal agent for Pickard's Mountain Eco-Institute, a remarkable project that runs pastured pork, and free range chickens, and a market garden, and a small biodiesel operation, and a micro wind turbine, and a tracking solar array, and some fascinating intern housing out of yurts and yomes and other cool structures.

And Abundance became the fiscal sponsor of the Sustainable Biodiesel Summit, and it started staging the "Biodiesel Intensive" workshops that were once held by Solar Energy International. Abundance launched a workshop series on everything from how to inoculate mushroom logs to how to make your own bread, to how to use worms to compost your food waste.

Under Tami's management it grew and thrived. Since it is a charity, it is not something that can be measured by "profits," but it can be measured by revenues, all of which are posted on its website with annual reports for every year. It can also be measured by Tami's salary, which started out as ten thousand a year, then edged up to twenty, then thirty, and when she received her first ever official "review" from the board compensation committee, she got a raise to thirty-five thousand dollars a year.

According to our Economic Development Corporation, the Chatham County average is twenty-nine thousand dollars a year. Tami has taken Abundance from zero to above average, and she has managed to hire help from folks like Camille and Jaime along the way.

One of the remarkable accomplishments of the Abundance Foundation is its alignment with the international Pecha Kucha movement. Pecha Kucha is a presentation style that emanates from the design community in Japan. It was introduced to us by long-standing board member Gary Phillips as an idea, and the folks at Abundance turned it into reality.

When I give speeches I tend to stay away from PowerPoint. I find it to be the death of public speaking. People who have no business standing in front of an audience feel qualified because they can make some PowerPoint slides. Which they tend to read slowly, while the audience waits.

PowerPoint is painful.

The creators of Pecha Kucha understand that implicitly. They invented a Japanese presentation style that involves twenty seconds per slide, times twenty slides. So each presentation is six minutes and forty seconds. Period. If you are not done saying your piece during a slide, tough. It moves without you. Which makes you look foolish, and makes you catch up, thereby forcing you to deliver a tight presentation.

What the Japanese did to trees with bonsai, and what they did to poetry with haiku, they have now done to PowerPoint, in the form of Pecha Kucha.

I believe the translation for the term is "the art of conversation," and the format has taken the world by storm. In London tickets to these events are sold out a year in advance. In most big cities Pecha Kucha is hard to get into.

And thanks to Abundance, Pecha Kucha has come to Pittsboro, making it the smallest center in the Pecha Kucha universe.

Talk about community development. On Pecha Kucha night, fifty or sixty enthusiasts will show up to hear ten six-minute-and-forty-second presentations. About anything. It might be about design. Or it might be about your horse farm. We've had presentations about HVAC, about courtyards, about sustainability, and about just about everything in between.

Under Tami's careful management, Abundance has built a significant brand. It was out early, and often with messages about sustainability, and it has grown at a managed rate.

When Habitat for Humanity needed an event planned, they hired Abundance. When Abundance sourced local food and intended to use real plates and glassware, Habitat balked at the price and muscled in with Styrofoam and a menu filled with far-away foods. At that point Abundance walked away, staying clear with their message of sustainability to the core — even if it is for Habitat for Humanity, a cause that is easy to believe in.

In the end Habitat came back to Abundance, and a "sustainable event" was had by all.

While that is a small thing, it is critically important. It matters to the local farmer who gets a nice order from a local organization, and it mattered to the Habitat management team — giving them a chance to think differently about their approach to feeding their volunteers.

When the Economic Development Corporation hired Abundance to help stage an event, the influence was also felt. Locally grown tomato plants graced every table, with one lucky winner getting to take one home. And Abundance co-produced a slide show with images of Chatham County commerce that included small-scale potteries and family farms and artisanal operations that are frequently left out of the economic development conversation.

In her speech from the stage, Diane Reed, our newly hired Economic Development Director tackled the subject head on — recognizing both large and small endeavors that were under way in our economy.

Again, it's a little thing. But it matters. There was a time in Chatham County when you had to be a multi-million dollar maker of particleboard in order to matter to the county's leaders. That's begun to shift, and Abundance has played a role in changing the conversation.

I sat in as an advisor on an Abundance board meeting in the early of winter of 2009, which was a time in history when the whole world was going "green." The "green" emphasis in the Obama administration's stimulus package made people come out of the woodwork to line up for handouts. People who had never even contemplated sustainability positioned themselves as experts. And the entire conversation in America began to change. What emerged at the board meeting was the notion that Abundance had been promoting a vision of "green" sustainable development for years. Abundance was funding energy audits of the Town of Pittsboro before anyone had even heard the word "stimulus."

Which means Abundance has contributed to the changing dialog in our community, and continues to lead on some fronts.

In early 2010 Abundance took occupancy of its "Office of the Future" which was a project that accidentally gained a lot of attention.

It began at Chatham Marketplace, where Matt Rudolf chastised me for not making office space available for his project, which was the North American office of the Roundtable for Sustainable Biofuels. Matt was formerly the executive director of Piedmont Biofuels Cooperative, which he left to work on the development of a global standard for sustainable fuels. He became a policy guy. With an office on the other side of town. And he longed to get inside the fence of our eco-industrial park.

We didn't have any office space available for Matt, and I came home from that lunch despondent. I walked across the campus and spotted the "sleep shack" that Jeff and a cadre of volunteers had built for Piedmont Biofarm. It was a delightful ten-foot by ten foot building, with a chalet like roof that had been built on a sled so that it could one day move into its rightful position somewhere on the farm.

The idea was that it was to provide shade and comfort for farm workers in the noonday sun. It was built in a low spot, and was unfinished, and as unfinished wooden structures are apt to do in North Carolina, it was starting to mold.

I walked down to the sleep shack and found it being used to store Jack and Adah's laundry, and some corn that they had grown. Not quite abandoned — but certainly not a proper deployment of resources. I thought it could be converted into a fine office, so I went to Doug to enquire about purchasing it.

We figured out how much the farm had invested in the sleep shack, agreed on a price, and the next day it was mine. Once I had "clear title," I hooked up a pair of tractors, and with the help of Russell and Jeremy, we slowly pulled it out of its low spot into a prominent position in the back yard, where it took its place on our former soccer field.

That's when I learned that what Jeff Gannon, the designer and the builder of the sleep shack, really wanted to do was open a new construction business called "Green Door Design." He wanted to deploy super insulated, small, moveable structures from appropriate materials, that could provide shelter and comfort.

Jeff was merely a like-minded individual who I had never met who was working away on the other side of the fence. The wood that went into the creation of the sleep shack had come from 30 miles away. The windows were the latest in tightness and efficiency.

And so we hired Jeff to finish it as an office. He went down and pulled the permits, built a wonderful deck and ramp for handicap access, finished it off with locally milled cedar, and completed it as a masterpiece.

Abundance board member Rebekah Hren then came down and held a solar workshop and installed enough photovoltaic panels to provide electricity for notebook computers, a ceiling fan, a dehumidifier, and lights. The yard filled up with solar enthusiasts. We got an assist from the folks at Southern Energy Management, particularly Maria Kingery who was also on the Abundance board at the time, and word of the "Office of the Future" began to spread.

Rebekah's husband Stephen came out and led a workshop on solar wall construction, such that the office now takes its indoor heat, and sends it for a spin across a plexi-glass covered black wall, and back into the office. It's low technology, but it works great on sunny days. E.F. Schumacher, the grandfather of "appropriate technology" would be proud of the simplicity and elegance of Stephen's design.

Stephen and Rebekah are the authors of *The Carbon Free Home,* and have been longtime friends of our project. They wrote a piece on the "Office of the Future" for *Huffington Post,* which made the project travel far and wide:

The Abundance Foundation's "Office of the Future".

"We recently had the pleasure of taking the battle against fossil fuels out of the home and into the workplace. The Abundance Foundation, a local non-profit focusing on all aspects of sustainability, was in cramped quarters with the space they share with Piedmont Biofuels, the fine folks down in Chatham County, North Carolina who are taking the waste stream of used restaurant oil and turning into a renewable fuel for our cars and trucks. So Abundance decided to venture out. Not too far, just into the yard, so they could still share the same kitchen, library, and other facilities they'd been using, but enough room to stretch their legs and contemplate the wide world of pepper varieties being grown by Doug Jones and the rest of the crew at Piedmont Biofarm."

We have been billing it as the first "actually green" office building in Chatham County, and it has caught the attention of those folks who teach the Green Building program at Central

Carolina Community College on the other side of town. Which means we have now added green building students to the list of people who occasionally come on tour.

At the rate we are going, tours are going to take a full afternoon rather than an hour. Bob built some container gardens out of old totes, which sit in the yard next to Abundance, so Tami and Camille and others can enjoy year-round arugula and greens from miniature greenhouses off their porch. I'm guessing there will be a square foot gardening workshop staged in the spring, modeling yet another way for local food to come into the world.

To measure the success of a charity we lack the typical yardstick of "profit." Since it is not designed to make a profit, we can measure it by growth. Abundance has grown from an idea at the table (or perhaps in the hot tub) to a quarter-million-dollar-a-year enterprise, and its influence has been felt across the state. In 2008 they were asked to consult with the North Carolina Center for Non-Profits on how they could reduce the ecological footprint of their annual conference.

Whether it is measured by growth, or influence, or the number of projects completed, Abundance has performed beautifully. Interestingly enough, by the end of 2009 Abundance had yet to land a single grant. They had tried on many occasions, but they had yet to find favor with the givers of public money grants.

Instead they were funded by programs, and donations from individuals, and from small bequests from family foundations. At age 13, Owen Fitzgerald was required by his family to donate a portion of his annual income to charity, which would be dutifully matched by his grandmother. And Owen has chosen Abundance as his charity for the past two years in a row.

One of the many fun stories to emanate from the history of the Abundance Foundation is that of Margaret Jemison, an heiress who is interested in everything from sustainable farming to dance and the arts. She was a former student of Doug Jones, and when she came for a plant tour, she was struck by the work he was doing on the genetics of pepper plants.

She donated a nice sum of money to Abundance, to support Doug's work, and one of the outcroppings was a large, delicious yellow pepper variety which Doug named "The Sweet Jemison." One of my favorite rites of late summer is to run a handful of Sweet Jemisons out to Margaret's house in the woods. Margaret has since gone on to underwrite some of the renewal of Saxapahaw.

A sidebar to Margaret's donation is microfinance. Donations often come into Abundance which are restricted. That is, they are to be released to a specific activity. In the case of monies from the Rollander Family Foundation, they were to be allocated to children's tours. In Margaret's case, the funds were to go to Doug's seed research.

Which means Abundance occasionally has money sitting around in the bank that is waiting to be deployed. With the guidance and approval of the board, Tami contacted a subset of her donors and suggested that she would like to loan out restricted funds on a demand basis, bearing interest, such that the money could not only earn something more than it was fetching at the bank, but also provide some much needed finance for projects that were in keeping with the mission of Abundance.

The Abundance donors completely understood the concept and agreed, which freed Tami up to make microloans from restricted funds, with the understanding to debtors that the money would be immediately returned on demand. Typically, restricted funds are released when certain milestones are achieved. In the case of Doug's seed saving, for instance, Margaret's money came into Abundance, a contract was drawn up between Abundance and Piedmont Biofarm, and money was released over time as milestones were achieved. Those monies that are not released, are restricted to Doug's project, but while they wait for the next milestone, they are lent out to do some work somewhere else.

And so Abundance entered the world of microfinance. The best example which leaps to mind is the expansion of Eastern Carolina Organics, who needed another drive-in cooler in order for their business to grow. They are the anchor tenant in Building 1, with some office space and a pair of coolers and a shared loading dock that is available to everyone in the park.

ECO was the first recipient of the Abundance Revolving Loan Program, and they helped craft the scope and scale. In an email and attached promissory note, ECO spelled it out to prospective lenders:

You'll see in the attached Promissory Note that we will be paying a flat rate of 5.25% (which is better than most savings accounts) and can return the funds within 45 days of written notice. This is non-compounding and we will pay off all interest fees annually, plus provide 1099-INT tax forms to keep it all official.

For purposes of record-keeping we can only accept contributions of $5,000 or MORE. If anyone agrees to contribute a loan, please fax/email this attached document for them to sign and mail in with their check.

If you come across someone looking for a tax-deductible donation, we can also receive a grant through our awesome neighbors, the Abundance Foundation.

She went on to include this snapshot of their business:

ECO was started to support the customers who were interested in buying larger volumes and more consistent supplies of organic produce grown by local NC farmers. We take all of the coordination and delivery pressure off of both the growers and the buyers, and we do all that legwork for them so the buyers can just place an order, like they do with all their conventional suppliers, and the growers can focus on their farms and not have to worry about things like negotiating on price, and making sure that they get paid, and staying on top of innovations in produce marketing. We want the growers to be able to take a step back from all that legwork and really focus on their soil, and their plants, and their own personal sustainability.

❀ ❀ ❀

We started ECO to see if people were going to "put their money where their mouth was," if they were going to be as committed to North Carolina organic farmers as their bumper stickers and their marketing brochures had communicated.

Our company is partly owned by the growers, and this unique partnership between growers and managers enables ECO to return 80% of the sales price back to the grower, plus a profit distribution to owners at the end of the year.

PROMISSORY NOTE

For VALUE RECEIVED, Eastern Carolina Organics, LLC (the undersigned, jointly and severally) promises to pay to _____ the principal sum of _____. Interest will be paid at the annual flat rate of 5.25%. Interest shall be paid annually. The said principal shall be payable in full in lawful money of the United States of America within two years of the date received. Loan maturity date can be extended with both parties agreement. Upon written request, monies will be repaid (in part or full) within 45 days from date of notice.

Eastern Carolina Organics, LLC _____

Date_____

Lender _____

Date_____

Lender's SSN_____

(ECO will provide annual tax forms)

We're trying to build a more sustainable, secure marketplace for consumers and growers through strong relationships and the belief that local farmers CAN provide wholesale volume and great quality.

Since beginning operations in 2004, we have reported profits for 2 out of 3 years, and sales have grown over 18% annually. 2008 is certain to set a record, as April 2008 was up 200% over April 2007. We expect sales to surpass $1.2m, yet still provide a maximum return to the grower, which keeps ECO's operational budget tight during these years of high capital growth. To date, we have successfully stayed cash-flow positive year-round while self-financing almost all of our expenses.

Accordingly as ECO grows, so does ECO's need for professional handling and storage of crops. We have paid off our first 2 coolers in full and just broke ground on a third big cooler which is a significant enough investment to meet our needs for 3 years (we think!). The project will cost $120,000 and we have self-financed $48,000 to date. We are looking to raise the balance by July 1 to complete the project.

ECO raised the money they needed, built the cooler, and expanded their business accordingly. This was one of many micro-finance projects that took root on our project, especially when we entered 2009 — the year the banks stopped lending.

In *Small is Possible*, I explored a variety of topics with chapter headings like "Feeding Ourselves" and "Fueling Ourselves." In the area of "Financing Ourselves," I gave our community particularly low marks. But today, the growth of Abundance can be attributed to its fiscal sponsorships, its well managed programs, and its ability to deliver on donor- advised projects. It's a remarkable story to have in our midst, and it is a wonderful companion to have at our side as we stumble along together, toward a sustainable future.

On the Label, Label, Label

LABELING IS TOUGH.

On the one hand we are taught from an early age the dangers of "labeling people." And we quickly learn how when we do label people, we tend to get it wrong — the girl in the wheelchair in kindergarten, the one with the club foot, goes on to run track and field and becomes the most beautiful woman in town.

It's an easy concept to grasp. But at the same time we cannot shake the jingle,

If it says Libby's, Libby's, Libby's on the label, label, label,
then you will like it, like it, like it on your table, table, table.

And despite the fact that Libbys is a purveyor of highly processed unsustainable grub for us to eat, the jingle is implanted in my memory for life.

The poor old notion of "organic agriculture" has fallen victim to a label and can't seem to get a break. It arose from the hippie ecology movement in the seventies, presenting a different way of food production that eschewed chemical fertilizers and pesticides and reintroduced old methods of growing food.

Some took to it for health reasons, preferring compost to chemical soil additives. Some took to it for spiritual reasons, wanting to be off the petroleum-dependent chemical grid. Others took to it for energy reasons, taking a lead from Buckminster Fuller, who suggested we should live off our solar income rather than squander our fossil savings.

Whether it was hippie chicks, or energy fanatics, or health nuts, the organic food movement forged along and became a rapidly growing niche market. When it became large enough to be noticed by the USDA, it became defined, and regulated. It got a label. And when that happened, many folks felt that the organic movement had been compromised completely.

"USDA Certified Organic" became a label that many found meaningless. On their quest to appease the many competing interests which aided and abetted them, the USDA watered down the regulations on organic to the point of being pointless. The USDA Organic seal certifies "95%" organic, which allows room for complicated synthetic molecules to slip in. It's good to know that dioxin can be used, as long as it is less than 5% — just so that it gets us that mouth feel we all enjoy.

Organic purists — those who reinvented the space, those who raise calories from compost, read *Permaculture Activist,* and subscribe to newsletters from the Rodale Institute — are unimpressed when their vegetable oil is allowed to contain 5% hexane and still bear a USDA Organic label.

Which means the purists argue with the pragmatists and the label is fraught with peril, and there is an entire conversation swirling about ranging from vegetables grown on sewage sludge to acceptance of genetically modified materials in our food supply.

I come to the debate from an energy perspective, which means I generally think organic is better for planet earth. But I also try not to get confused. When I see people buying "organic" pickles from Oregon at Chatham Marketplace, I bury my head in my hands. Most of America's pickles come from Mount Olive, North Carolina, which is just down the road a piece.

And while Mount Olive may not bear the "organic" label, their product would be the clear choice from an energy perspective. And if you are an energy purist you might reflect on how we can't really eat pickles in the first place. The energy required to get that baby cucumber in the jar is way more than the calories returned. (Although I will admit, when I am outside of our bubble dining at local eateries in the Carolinas, I am sometimes glad to see pickles, since they can be the only green item on the menu.)

To their credit, Chatham Marketplace has also started labeling their produce with "Local," to make it easier for those of us attempting to dine on a hundred mile diet.

Clearly organic food production will be the defining attribute of food for the low carbon future. I prefer local, and "sustainable," which lacks a label, to "organic" which can easily come from New Zealand.

Nowhere is this quandary of words and labeling more evident than over at Eastern Carolina Organics. They are the anchor tenant of Building One, and they are the brainchild of the Carolina Farm Stewardship Association, which launched them with a grant from the Tobacco Trust Fund.

When big tobacco died on the stalk after it was revealed they had lied to regulators about the addictive nature of their product, duped consumers, and generally behaved in an underhanded fashion, they left town in a hurry. And along the way they left a giant pot of money behind.

The money was ostensibly for economic development in tobacco dependent counties, and some of it spawned Eastern Carolina Organics. That was a fantastic idea. ECO has grown, created jobs, and is an inspirational outlet for organic and sustainably produced food.

One of the unfortunate myths which circulates in the sustainable agriculture community, is that the "middle man" must be eliminated whenever possible. I think the notion has been borrowed from conventional agriculture and is consistently misapplied by agricultural extension agents — and sustainable farming advocates — everywhere.

While it might be true that commodity corn production gets sliced and diced so fine that the farmer fails to realize the value of their crop — by the time they pay one firm to transport it, and another to dry it, and another to store it, and another to mill it, and another to extract the fructose from it — it may very well be the case that most of that value fails to return to the farm.

But the logic does not hold true when it comes to ECO. By leaving 20% behind, most farmers could do the same amount of work, deliver their wares to ECO, and take the weekend off.

I watch the farmers labor, washing and packing and loading trucks and trailers into the night, and I see them depart at 6:00 in the morning to drive for hours to get to market when they could be simply dropping off product at the ECO coolers and sleeping late instead.

They are taught by the sustainable agriculture machine that they must go direct, but that's only because most food sheds do not have an ECO to work with.

One of the things that ECO does is stick to its mission, and that is, handling "organic" produce. With over a million dollars a year in revenue, they are the elephant in our food shed, dwarfing most sustainable farming operations by far. And they do sell non-organic product from time to time.

ECO is a market connector. They have the routes, and the refrigerated trucks, and the relationships with chefs to move product. They do sell some non-organic food — they are happy to support local and sustainable farms — but when they do that, they do it at market price, rather than the 80/20 split their members enjoy.

That means that if a grower has a few tons of sweet potatoes, they can go to Sandi and she might try to find a home for their crop. If sweet potatoes are trading at $3.00 a pound, and she needs to beat the California price to play, she might offer a 50% discount to the grower.

Farmers who take such a deal, walk away thinking they would be better off at a farmers market selling their sweet potatoes directly.

What is less clear is that if they would simply certify to be organic, demonstrate to ECO that they could consistently deliver high quality product on time, and join their ranks, the discount would fall to 20% and be a vastly superior deal.

I'm not a farmer. I'm merely an eater. But I have helped spawn a couple of farm enterprises, and I have jumped in with Jason and Haruka over at Edible Earthscapes.

Jason and Haruka joined us from Japan and took over the farm at Piedmont Biofuels Coop that Doug had started. It had a splendid 90- foot greenhouse and about a half acre of dirt, and it was just slightly too small to provide a living. It needed some space. I had two acres of fallow, cleared land adjoining their farm on the other side of the creek. We both understood it would take capital to install a fence, and an irrigation system, and to bring the soil back to life.

And we understood it would take a lot of work and expertise to make it happen. I had the land and the capital, and because I was able to wait patiently for a return, I wanted to invest in a long term crop.

Jason and I talked it over, and our journey began with Sandi. We met with her to find out what was involved in organic certification, and perhaps more importantly, to find out what we should venture into.

Organic certification is a piece of cake. It costs around $500, of which about half can easily be clawed back from the government. It is about record-keeping, and crop rotation, and about having a plan and sticking with it. For the organized farmer, it is not a very high bar.

Trace Ramsey, the anarchist at Circle Acres farm is a registered organic certifier, and agreed to take Jason's organic expansion on.

With the organic part within reach, the question remained of what to grow. I wanted to go into perennials, since I notice most of the local growers are in annuals. Most growers are short on cash, and have to take off an annual crop in order to stay a float. Our cash crops tend to be things like sweet potatoes, or peppers, or garlic.

But I wanted to go into a long term play — something that would take a while to establish, and would yield for many years. Sandi said she would buy every stick of organic asparagus we could harvest. Bingo. We decided to go long on asparagus.

So Edible Earthscapes and I have started down the long journey to asparagus. Step one was the deer fence. We used cedar poles rather than pressure-treated, since pressure-treated would contravene organic certification — besides, I'm guessing pressure-treated wood will be banned during my lifetime.

Step two was to kill the grass. Jason ran a chisel plow over the fenced-in field to break up the sod, then ran the discs over it. Then tilled it. Over and over. Each time the Johnson grass was fixing to reroot, he was there disrupting its growth cycle with a tiller. Rather than spraying toxic herbicides, he was doing it with mechanical power — run on 100% biodiesel. Any way you slice it, if you are going to convert a fallow field into a productive field, hydrocarbons will be deployed. It's just a matter of where those hydrocarbons come from.

Step three was to plant a cover crop. Jason chose buckwheat, and transformed the field into a remarkable show of white flowers. Buckwheat was fixing nitrogen, and taking over, and shading the soil, and was tilled under before setting seed.

Step four is creating the beds. Then we will plant the crowns. Then we will tend the asparagus patch. And it will spend an entire year developing its root system. Which means we will be careful not to harvest anything. The second year we might be able to harvest a bit. Not market quantities, but rather, neighborhood quantities. And in year three we will hit pay dirt.

A well-managed asparagus patch should yield for fifteen years. Once it comes into its own it will generate tens of thousands of dollars per year from a single acre, which Jason and I will split. As investors in the project, we will see a return on my money and Jason's labor in three years.

Small investments, small returns. It is a myriad of plays like this that have formed the backbone of our project. This one happens to be gambling on "organic," and will put us squarely in business with Eastern Carolina Organics, which means we will never want for customers, nor need to rise early for journeys to faraway market stalls.

The labeling dilemma is not limited to food, of course. For years the notion of how to create a label for sustainable biodiesel has been circulating around the industry. If I had a nickel for every hour I have spent writing about it, talking about it, and sitting in on conference calls about it, I could be retired right now.

Having been intimately involved in a "labeling process," I see how immediately tricky it becomes, which makes me want to cut the USDA some slack. Give me a shot of hexane. I'll chase it down with some locally brewed beer.

In the biodiesel space, gigantic food interests get involved. In Europe, the primary feedstock for biodiesel is rapeseed, the North American equivalent of which is canola. In America, the primary constituent for biodiesel is soy — which isn't really even an oilseed crop. We don't grow soy for the oil — which has the fat we use to make fuel. We grow it for the protein — which is in the meal that we feed to animals.

Regardless of this, Big Soy pulls up a seat at the "Sustainable Biodiesel" table and throws its weight around. Hard core activists want to start by saying "Soy is unsustainable. We can't grow soy for fuel."

And when Big Soy replies, "Why not make fuel out of those soybeans that are growing all around you? Why not help the farmers who are struggling right now? Why not make your fuel out of product from within 100 miles of your biodiesel plant?"

It's an argument that presents Sustainable Biodiesel with a problem. Sustainable Biodiesel wants to protect rainforests from being destroyed to plant more soy. So it wants to rule out soy-based biodiesel from its sustainability label, and the language it uses is "indirect land use patterns."

Makes sense. We don't want the biodiesel industry in America to become so lucrative through the use of virgin soybean oil that we motivate farmers in the developing world to replace the rainforest with soy.

But what about the coastal plain of North Carolina? The environmental destruction of growing soy down there occurred many generations ago. Should we use that cleared, degraded land to sink some carbon and create some livelihoods to replace petroleum, or should it be ruled out of the label?

It's complicated. Labeling efforts have transformed the way we consume coffee. In my life time coffee has gone from a straight commodity product to "shade grown, organic, fair trade," and consumers have noticed the switch. The change in the coffee industry's industrial practices has been good for the land, for migratory birds, and has elevated the standard of living for coffee workers.

And labeling efforts have changed our relationship to seafood. We now have a preference for "dolphin safe" tuna.

And while all of these might be merely niche markets, from fair trade to organic, to dolphin safe, they are where the growth is. Our society is shifting to a preference for ecological stewardship, and those businesses that can get outside of business as usual, whether it be with a label, or by transforming their practices, will be the winners in the low carbon future.

15

Solar Double Cropping

FOR AS LONG as I can remember, my brothers and I have gathered together one or two times a year for what we call "Brother's Weekend." In the beginning it was an exotic adventure in which we would perpetually try to "one up" one another.

Glen would plan a canoe trip to Algonquin Park in northern Ontario. I would book a sailing junket off the coast of North Carolina; Jim would rent a houseboat and take us on a fishing expedition. We would mostly play cards, and laugh, and update one another with the state of our respective businesses, and lives, and most importantly we would bat ideas around.

Over the years the exotic gave way to the commonplace. We no longer needed to go kayaking on the French Broad. All we needed was a card table, and a pack of cards, and we could fabricate a fantastic inspirational weekend in which we would generally laugh longer and harder than we did at any other time of the year.

On one nondescript weekend in Lion's Head, Ontario, Jim and Glen and I were walking along Isthmus Bay road, with frequent glimpses of Georgian Bay, and were discussing the new feed-in tariff for solar electricity generators in Ontario.

Policy changes present opportunities. Since both Glen and I are immersed in the renewable energy business, we understand the importance of policy decisions on the relative prosperities of our enterprises.

As the three of us were walking down the road, Glen explained that Ontario had recently passed a law that restricted lucrative solar farms on high quality farmland.

Oops. That's food versus fuel, again. And as someone in the biodiesel business, I know that this one always ends badly for the fuel.

I've written about this subject extensively. In *Biodiesel Power* I missed the point entirely, focusing on how hunger was not about the production of calories, but rather, about inadequacies in our food distribution system. I played off the notion that "on one side of the fence there is a hungry family, and on the other side of the fence there is a Dumpster full of food."

But as I walked along with my brothers, listening to Glen describe the new law limiting solar arrays, the entire debate washed over me once again.

I did not want the solar industry to encounter the same bruising ride. And after talking about it for awhile Glen suggested that it might be possible to grow food beneath a utility scale solar array.

At which point I embarked on the long journey of what I referred to as Solar Double Cropping. I wrote about it in Energy Blog:

Blog

Wind energy gets all the breaks when it comes to interfacing with farmers. After all, farmers can get lease payments from turbines on their land, while raising contented cows on the fields below.

This "double cropping" relationship is in the wind industry's favor. Solar is not so lucky. Solar farms typically displace valuable farmland. Which is why there are some jurisdictions, like Ontario, where legislation is appearing to ban the use of solar on class 1 and class 2 farmland.

Step one: put in place a valuable feed-in tariff so that renewable energy is economically attractive. The market will respond with thousands of acres of solar panels — possibly wiping out wine country — because the energy policy dictates that electricity is now more valuable than wine.

Step two: ban solar farms on farmland in order to protect wine country.

If it were up to me, I would wipe the chalkboard clean and rethink.

How do we grow food beneath solar arrays? From my limited understanding of food production, I think there are lots of ways:

As our agricultural zone changes (we are moving from zone 7 to zone 8 in my part of North Carolina), we see heat pressure on some of our crops. Little things, like lettuce and arugula. Climate change dictates that some crops will vacate North Carolina in the years to come. We are already seeing some benefits from a little shade. Which means we ought to be able to leverage some solar shade to continue to produce crops.

Protecting plants from water on their leaves is a good way to stave off disease. Those growers with the finest (and longest lasting) tomatoes tend to shelter their plants from water. That is, they create a desert environment and deliver water only to the roots of the plants. Call it season extension in the land of the diseased. Why not shelter the plants with solar cells?

Lots of plants need structures to thrive. At Piedmont Biofarm all of the peppers are trellised. Unlike the peppers in my garden, which fall over and get eaten by critters. Surely we could leverage off the structures needed for solar panels to reduce our investment in pepper trellises.

These days giant solar arrays make great investments for those with tax liabilities. Having lost my fortune in biodiesel, I don't have any tax liabilities. But just because I don't owe the taxman, doesn't mean someone else couldn't benefit from investing in a solar double cropping play.

I've been thinking about this for awhile now. And today the phone rang with an excited investor who wants to see the grand experiment move forward. Today we received a commitment for a 100Kw array at the plant.

That's big. I have a 2Kw array in my yard. Sometimes it generates as much electricity as my family consumes. This project will be 50 times the size. It will be grid-tied. And it will be designed and built with the notion of generating power above, and enhancing food production below.

Which just makes sense. As we charge headlong into a low carbon future we are going to need more energy, and more food. Rather than positioning one against the other, we need to integrate the two.

And today everyone on project is jazzed about our opportunity to design and build both. Standby for an acre or two of blue panels popping up at the plant...

By the time I submitted the idea to the Buckminster Fuller Institute I was much more concise. I wrote:

In the future we will need more energy. And more food. Pitting solar electricity production against food is both silly and dangerous.

If we accept climate change as the moral imperative of our time, we understand the urgent need to develop energy production from renewable, non-fossil sources.

Each year the Buckminster Fuller Institute issues a Challenge in which it seeks the best ideas on earth. My solar double cropping idea was dropped from the first round. Oh well. It didn't win a prize. But we are going to build it anyway.

As we were working on the design for our solar double cropping project, we cut up two totes as container gardens and outfitted them with a "semi-shade" panel that has its silicon solar collectors printed on glass. It takes 50% of the light energy which strikes it for use as electricity, and lets 50% of the light energy hit the plants below. While it is a moveable prototype that we can easily disassemble and take around to demonstrate the concept (growing lettuce while powering an iPod), it is also providing electricity to our Pittsboro fueling station.

I once had the pleasure of traveling to Bear Island, off the coast of Maine, to spend some time with the descendents of Buckminster Fuller. They regaled me with stories of how everyone would gather at the kitchen house for a community dinner, after which Uncle Bucky would stand up and deliver a three-hour lecture on whatever was on his mind.

I'm guessing he would give a nod to solar double cropping — even if his current board of trustees are inundated with superior ideas.

Our Place in the World

I ONCE WAS INVITED to a meeting of the Southern Growth Policies Board, which is a right-wing think tank, created by a group of regional governors to support the status quo. They meet under the guise of economic development and pretend that they have some value in the world.

I attended one of their posh luncheons, and dined with a young economic developer out of Boone, North Carolina, who explained to me under his breath that the "South is where industry goes to die."

It's not something you want to whisper when the kind people of Southern Growth are feeding you, but he was completely right. A few key levers — all of which are hallmarks of the status quo — characterize economic development in the South.

We offer cheap electricity. It's not because we have abundant hydro-power from rivers. Nor is it that we capture even a small percentage of our abundant sunlight. Rather, it comes from coal, which we subsidize through a regulated utility system. So we are cheap. Electricity is so cheap there is no need to shut your lights off when you are not using them.

We offer cheap labor. Not only do we have an undereducated workforce living in trailers with confederate flags on their license plates, but we are a "right to work" state, which means our courts tend to heavily favor the employer. In North Carolina you can fire someone for the way they wear their hair. And if they sue, the courts will rule it as "just cause."

We have some brainpower. Parts of North Carolina are populated with highly educated folks who seldom go to watch NASCAR on weekends.

All of which amounts to a culture where industry stops for a time, before moving to the developing world. We saw this with textiles. And furniture. And tobacco. And nowadays we are seeing it with the technology crowd. We wooed Dell to come to Winston-Salem, and they came for a time to gobble up tax credits, and they left before developing the high tech workforce they promised.

My friend Gary Thompson tells me that Microsoft is having a hard time locating programming talent in America these days, and has started opening development centers in China. Apparently American kids are better at playing video games than they are at creating them.

North Carolina did manage to land Google in Caldwell County. They wanted the unsightly railroad tracks removed from their view shed, and the government complied. Too bad about Randy's biodiesel plant that was just down the road apiece. Randy was counting on rail access to move his renewable fuel to market. I'm guessing Google chose North Carolina for our cheap electricity. The energy consumption on their server farms is legendary.

Twisting the lens a bit, to focus more on Chatham County, North Carolina, we find a fascinating place that has been sharply divided for generations. On the western side of the county is Siler City, which is known for its conservative politics, and its chicken processing plants, and subsequently its immigrant community.

Siler City has gained national recognition several times, once when David Duke came to town to address a crowd of enthusiastic white supremacists, and on the *Andy Griffith Show.*

On one episode, when Barney Fife is locking up Otis, the town drunk, Otis complained that if the service in Mayberry's jail did not improve he was "going to take his business to Siler City." And it is Siler City, after all, where Aunt Bee chose to retire.

On the eastern side of the county is Pittsboro, the county seat, which is known for its artists, and hippies, and progressive politics. The best farmland in Chatham County was in the eastern part of the county in the New Hope River Valley, which was dammed for the creation of Jordan Lake. Those on the eastern side of the county fought the lake, and those on the western side of the county supported the lake because they wanted the water for their industries.

The great irony is that most of the thirsty industries of Siler City left town a long time ago, but the bitterness of the lake struggle still informs the collective thinking.

The divide in Chatham County's community doesn't end with politics or the creation of the lake. It goes much deeper than that. A greater schism exists between "old" versus "new."

"Old Chatham" tends to share the stereotypical values of the American southland, which is fiercely independent, religious in nature, suspicious of government, and interested in self-preservation. It's a place where pickup trucks have gun racks, and convenience stores have sales on ammunition, and bumper stickers sport confederate flags and read "Heritage, Not Hate."

Newcomers to the county often tend to be more educated, less independent, less religious, more comfortable with government, and interested in societal change. Retirees from the north in search of mild winters, golfing enthusiasts, and those associated with nearby Research Triangle Park tend to form the core of the "New Chatham" demographic.

Which means we have trailer parks nestled up against gated golf course communities. And the values of each occasionally clash.

One of the fascinating phenomena to note is the way the "newcomers" tend to have an anti-development bent. That's after they have moved in. Once someone gets their piece of paradise, they are suddenly highly concerned with limiting the growth of others who might despoil it.

With the advent of Depression 2.0, many housing developers left town, or went belly up, or walked away from their projects all together. Housing tracts designed for 1,200 sit virtually empty, with an elaborate stone entrance and six houses. The $10 million butterfly center that was to anchor "The Parks" is now just a falling-down billboard. Like the George Carlin sketch, most of the developments were named for things they were replacing: Fox Run getting its name from the bulldozer driver who turned over a fox burrow, and Frog Pond from the fact that there were once frogs in the neighborhood — before they dyed the pond water to improve the aesthetic about the place.

In her front page article in the *Independent Weekly,* Rebecca Cowell referred to Chatham County as "Zombieland," after vast developments where the trees were pushed down for roads that were never finished.

Which means the "anti-development" crowd is happy, for the time being, and those nature lovers in our midst enjoy more than their fair share of natural capital, but if the market comes back, we will face being flattened by housing starts again.

Our role in this place is a funny one. I can't help but think of Harm de Blij's *The Power of Place,* and of how I will never quite fit into this culture I have adopted as my own.

Our 14-acre campus is surrounded by barbed wire that is covered with 30 years of abandoned honeysuckle. We are a large project by local standards, employing as many as 70 people across multiple businesses and properties. And as such we are both loved and reviled.

Those who love us are those who are excited by our demographic. Our project tends to be populated by young, big-brained, passionate people which bring a much needed vitality to the town.

A local record label, Trekky Records, holds an annual festival in the yard at the Plant.

We have twenty-somethings renting the Community House to throw dance jams, and hosting bands at the Plant and the Mill, and throwing Mardi Gras parties. The City Tap, a new, hip watering hole downtown thrives when it is payday at the Plant. Our mayor, Randy Voller, understands this. No stranger to the partying life himself, he has embraced our demographic, often welcoming our interns into his home for parties of his own.

Others do not. Our Town Board hates us. To many we are a bunch of dirty hippies with weird ideas, running around on that funny-smelling fuel, and taking money from the government that should be rightfully left in the pockets of the taxpayers. My friend Chris Jude lived in Pittsboro for a time, and moved to Seattle to become a solar installer. When he returned to work at Piedmont Biofuels a couple of years later he remarked, "The only difference between this town and any other small town in America is there are a lot more old Mercedes diesels." And I think he is right about that. Generally when I see an old Mercedes coming toward me on the highway it is one of our members and I get a wave.

Most of the "haters" have no idea what we are actually about. They don't tend to read our books, or our blogs, but rely instead on word of mouth, which can sometimes get a little twisted and unreliable.

All we are doing is trading amongst ourselves. And with others. It's a concept that is surely as old as the human race. Whether we exchange goods or services with PLENTYs (our local currency), or federal reserve banknotes, or time with one another, is irrelevant. We are simply exercising the freedom to trade.

In his book, *Life Inc.*, Douglas Rushkoff talks about how the overwhelming majority of humanity is engaged in a "virtual economy" that leaves them marginalized and devoid of meaning. The over-corporatized society Rushkoff explores does not permit the average person to create value in the economy. And he is right about that. Our project operates in what Rushkoff would call a "real economy," in which you hug the woman who grew the pork you are carrying home in a box.

To my surprise, the other thing Rushkoff claims is that projects like ours are the solution to saving human society in general. When his hardcover first edition had run its course and he was going into paperback, he asked me to contribute something about our project so that his readers could get a sense of where to start. Here is what I wrote:

blog

We've made a lot of mistakes at Piedmont Biofuels. We've never had a plan. We began with a handful of passionate individuals making biodiesel out of used cooking oil in the back yard. Biodiesel is a cleaner-burning renewable fuel that can run any diesel engine. And it can easily be made in the corner of the garage.

We were "homebrewers." And what we wanted was more gallons.

But we were wrong about that.

Many biodiesel cooperatives have formed and folded. Many biodiesel collectives have come and gone. People fall to fighting, money comes to the fore, and someone takes their reactor and goes home. Things fall apart. If all we had to deal with was renewable energy — just BTUs — it would be simple. But because there are people involved, it's trickier.

Piedmont Biofuels is still together. We went from a backyard brewing setup, to a cooperative fuel making operation, to a million-gallon-per-year chemical plant. We accidentally created a model for community-scale biodiesel, in which Moya collects used cooking oil from area restaurants, Jeremy spins it into fuel, Xiaohu certifies that it conforms to our specification, and I put it on a truck and deliver it to the B100 Community Trail, where hundreds of long-suffering members fill up their cars and trucks. We sell the rest to oil companies, who blend it with petroleum and sell our product to thousands of consumers across the region.

People used to ask us how we managed to stick together, and we always used to tell them that we tried to do what was in the best interest of the fuel. And while it is true that many of us have subjugated our self-interest in the name of the fuel, I think we had that part wrong.

It's not about the gallons. It's not about the fuel. It's about people.

We envisioned a world in which the stuff we needed to make our fuel would come from within 100 miles of our plant, and where the fuel would be sold within that same 100 miles. It's easy. We simply wanted to upend the overarching, top-down energy infrastructure that ruled our lives. We wanted to get free of the petroleum grid. We saw a world of micro-nodal energy production, where energy would be harnessed at the place it was used. That's all.

We accidentally formed a relationship between people and their fuel. Which meant we formed relationships with a larger group — those of us who cared about our fuel.

It wasn't about the gallons. It was about the people who wanted the gallons for motive power.

We made the same mistake when it came to food.

When you are obsessed with the production of local fuel, it is a small step to focus on local food. So we formed a farm in the front yard. And when we wanted to expand food production we launched another farm in town, on the vacant lot that surrounds our chemical plant.

When we were shipping trucks and trailers full of food, we thought it was about sustenance. We mistakenly believed it was about growing calories. But in fact it was about interacting with those people who were intent on eating locally produced, sustainable food.

On our quest for sustainable biodiesel, we found ourselves immersed in ways to improve the "energy balance" of our fuel. We had fuel-makers who were riding their bikes to work, and we obsessed over the "life cycle analysis" of our plant. That aligned us squarely with the solar installation community, as we deployed solar thermal and photovoltaic systems to get our work done.

Along the way we took on like-minded tenants. One of which was distributing organically grown produce. Another started making non-toxic bug repellant using biodiesel as its start point.

Suddenly we were what the economic developers call a "cluster," and with seventy-some-odd people employed on our project, we were having a material impact on our small southern town's economy. One day I got a call from a gentleman at Standard and Poor's who wanted to talk to me about our county's credit rating. What? Because we had emerged from the community college, the county pointed to us as one of their successes, and wanted our existence to provide a demonstration of what they did with their debt instruments.

I said to Rachel, "Back when you and I were trying to make biodiesel for the first time, did we ever think it would lead to a role in public finance?"

She replied, "Probably. But at the time I just wanted you to add more lye..."

Seven years before there was a "stimulus package for green jobs," back in the first W. Bush administration, we were calling for an "energy regime change." One of our members coined the term "Hometown Security."

Having accidentally built critical mass in our small southern town, our interest in self-reliance increased. We were fueling ourselves. We were feeding ourselves. But we were having trouble financing ourselves.

In the spring of 2008 my book, *Small is Possible: Life in a Local Economy* hit the bookstores. In it I mentioned a local currency effort called the PLENTY — which was an acronym for Piedmont Local Economy Tender. It had nothing to do with us, really, except we traded in it. And we paid our interns with PLENTYs.

That book restarted an interest in the PLENTY, a new board of trustees was formed and the currency was re-launched with new vigor in the fall of 2008, just as the rest of the world was melting down. Our locally owned Capital Bank started accepting PLENTYs at par, and the headline: "Local Bank Accepts Local Currency" became international news.

Before we knew it we had film crews from Poland, and CNN, and Fox, and crews from shows that I had never heard of, like *Inside Edition,* running around our small town filming people spending PLENTYs at the grocery store.

I don't have a TV. And I don't get out much. But for a moment there we were big news.

Ironically, the PLENTY has a much smaller role in our local finance efforts than the peer-to-peer financing that also rose from an experiment I outlined in *Small is Possible.* I took ten thousand dollars of my kid's college savings and lent it to a local cabinetmaker at 4% so she could pay off her credit cards that were charging 28%.

And it worked. She got back on her feet. Microloans started popping up everywhere. When the "credit crunch" of 2009 set upon us, money started coming out of the woodwork. Landlords were lending to tenants for capital equipment necessary to keep small businesses alive. The Abundance Foundation started a revolving credit program out of static "restricted funds." Neighbors started lending to neighbors. Peer pressure is the glue that holds microfinance together. If I want to default on a loan from Mrs. Ferguson in this town, I best move away.

And the beauty of it is that 4% microloans have outperformed the S+P 500 of late.

Just as the fuel wasn't about the gallons, and the food wasn't about the calories, the local currency and the loans aren't about the money. They are about the people who use the money. For the new mechanic's garage. Or a new table saw. They are not even about the "stuff" the money can buy. They are about the human who is going to use the stuff to create a living.

We were once dubbed "the most exciting renewable energy project on the Eastern Seaboard." And while we liked the moniker, it was incorrect.

It turns out that everything we do is about people. And about how we interact with people. People just want to be in on things. And people just want to have a say in how they can govern their own lives. People just want to be supported. And cared for. And more importantly, people want to have something they can care about too.

At Piedmont Biofuels, we have encountered mental illness. We have felt the sting of departure from those who have moved on. We've faced death. And terminal illness. We've had parties and we've had births. We've had ribbon cuttings, and politicians speaking, and accidents and explosions, and potlucks and games tournaments, and quarrels over dogs and cats, and when all is said and done, when the last book is written, it's just about us. And how we hold together. As a project. And as people. Just trying to find our way…

We Are Not Alone

IN THE WINTER OF 2010 I was asked to speak to the Low Carbon Transportation Committee of the newly established North Carolina Energy Policy Council. And I was pleased. Pleased to have a government who "gets it," and pleased to be invited to speak.

I went down to the Department of Commerce, which is located in a giant pink granite-looking building near the legislature (those who work there refer to it as "The Pink Palace"), and I found my way to the conference room where the panel was meeting.

The "experts" included some guys from Piedmont Natural Gas who were arguing that they had the lowest carbon fuel, and lots of it, and they just needed some help to get it into our transportation fleet. They knew their stuff, and were impressive, though I noticed they had left biodiesel out of their charts showing the various carbon footprints of various fuels.

Anne Tazewell spoke. She's been a major player in alternative transportation policy-making for years. She has pushed boulder after boulder up mountains. We have occasionally worked together. Our styles are quite different. And our visions are often completely different. But after many years of grinding away on societal change, I have to say I have a deep and abiding respect for her and the work she does. She was an excellent choice to address the group.

Steven Burke from the North Carolina Biofuels Center was one of the presenters. He's remarkable. He gave a flashy slide show about imagination and decision-making, and how societal change happens. He chooses words we don't normally encounter and bandies them about effortlessly. He's not a nuts-and-bolts guy. I wouldn't want him holding a wrench. But few people can be as inspiring at the podium.

After we had all addressed the committee we had a freewheeling discussion which horrified me. The chairman didn't know the difference between biomass and biofuels and biotechnology. Or what we were doing there. Or why we would be concerned about carbon.

I was so distraught when I left the meeting that instead of driving to the plant I drove to Larry's Beans instead. One of the owners, Kevin, was glad to interrupt his day to wander around their coffee roasting operation to chat, and to show me his new inventions, and to calm me down.

Larry's Beans is a coffee roaster which has become obsessed with sustainability. They have renovated some crummy warehouses in a lousy part of town into the most spectacular coffee factory imaginable. Where there was once corrugated tin they have put in clerestory windows for daylighting. They have converted a drainage swale into a courtyard. And they have done it so artfully that it appears effortless.

When I showed up I explained to Kevin that I had just come from the policy world and I needed a dose of hope. I don't think Kevin does a lot of policy work. But as a pioneer I think he intrinsically understood my funk. He walked me over to his new rainwater collection system that he had plumbed in to flush his toilets. I was intrigued. I wanted one. His appeared to have been a prefabricated kit, using an electrically powered pump, and I knew as I was envying it that ours would be cobbled together by us and would use gravity instead. Why I am not flushing my toilets with rainwater is one of the great mysteries of this world.

Kevin was relieved to have completed some annual contract negotiations with one of their big customers, and was pleased to report an upturn in business in the dead of the winter. He complained that his sales were off at Chatham Marketplace, which I easily accounted for by explaining that I had recently abandoned my five cup a day habit and had stopped buying his product en masse for the plant kitchen.

He laughed it off and explained they were putting together a strategy to boost sales at the Marketplace.

One of the things I love about Larry's Beans is that they began with business as their platform, encountered sustainability as a concept, and as they embarked down the road of sustainability, they found it more interesting than the business itself. Or perhaps more challenging. And while pursuing their goals of transforming their operation into something that might demonstrate how a business could sustain human life on this planet, they found that the passion for sustainability was actually good for the business.

People want to buy from the sustainable coffee roaster. Coffee was one of the last items I cut from my 100 mile diet. I dined on foods that came from within 100 miles of my plate for years, but I allowed cheating, which meant I drank coffee. Cutting coffee from my diet brings me much closer to home. I understand that perhaps there is something intrinsically unsustainable about roasting coffee in Raleigh, North Carolina, but the mere fact that Kevin and Larry and company are giving it a go is a complete inspiration to a lot of people. They are not the biggest coffee roaster in the region, but they have made a mark on the industry.

And whether it is their decision to support fair trade or to buy from coffee cooperatives in the developing world, or whether it is pushing back on their supply chain to demand decent wages or to support fair prices for growers, or whether it means getting a loan from the State Energy Office to weatherize their plant, Larry's Beans is working on it with all they've got.

In *Powerdown*, Richard Heinberg writes of "Lifeboats," which are those businesses or organizations that will enable us to survive in a world of resource depletion. Heinberg can be a little grim for my taste, but I believe his notion of lifeboats is spot on.

What we need as we forge forward, often onto ground that has not yet been traveled, is examples of other companies who have successfully done what we are thinking about doing. In many ways that is all Piedmont Biofuels is. We are on a quest for community-scale biodiesel production, and we're demonstrating a lot of energy and sustainability stuff along the way.

Another company I turn to for inspiration is Southern Energy Management (SEM). In 2002, Bob Kingery was hawking solar thermal equipment out of the back of his car. He has since grown to become the largest solar installer in the state, with multiple offices, and a staff of technicians, energy auditors, engineers, and whatever else it takes to send solar collectors out in the world.

Bob runs the company with his wife, Maria, who is an inspiration in herself. They occupy a nondescript flex space by the airport, but when you enter it feels more like walking into a living room than a high-powered solar distribution office. Bob's desk is right next to Maria's, in the middle of the room, where everyone can see everyone. Its cozy. Inviting. Transparent.

When Southern Energy Management purchased a worm bin from us, they were told they would need a permit from the state in order to operate it. I doubted that, since they had no intention of selling their worm castings. They merely wanted to feed company food waste to the worms, and return the castings to the soil. Or to the gardens of their employees. Just the same, they decided to take a run at it, and engaged the state in whether or not an enterprise such as SEM would need a permit, and what that process might look like.

Those companies involved in business as usual would not take the time or expense to pursue such a thing. But Bob and Maria did. Because they felt it mattered. And they understand pioneering efforts — they are in the renewable energy business, harnessing the sun to heat hot water and homes and to make electricity for the grid. They do megawatt-scale systems, and have watched the industry mature before their eyes.

Many of us have tried hard to get Southern Energy Management to move out of their rented quarters and buy a place in Pittsboro so that we could be more closely connected. And while such a move might make some financial sense, they refuse, because it would dramatically increase the carbon footprint of their operation.

Down at the Plant, Abundance had a donor suggest that he really wanted to build a stirling engine. That's a mechanical device that lives off the delta between hot and cold. He told me that he wanted to buy an evacuated solar tube, or two, so that he could have a heat source for his prototype. I went to Southern Energy Management and explained the project. They gave me a couple of tubes, complete with manifold, all ready to go. It came out of their scrap heap. It appears it might have been for trade show demonstrations.

I delivered it to Nick, the stirling engine guy. He reached for his wallet, and was delighted to hear "no charge." Just as Southern Energy Management would dip into their "bone pile" to help me out, I frequently do the same for others. In my case it is usually in the form of drums or totes or pumps and things. We are like-minded companies. I buy solar gear from them from time to time, they run a portion of their fleet on our fuel, and we are connected in a myriad of ways. "Lifeline" or "lifeboat" might be a little strong, but we go beyond "network." Certainly we are linked by being in business together, but more so because of the steadfast belief that one another "gets it," and is working on a mission that is larger than simply lining our wallets.

Clothing Facts

Amount Per Shirt

	% Daily Values
Sweatshop Labor	0%
Pesticides Used	0%
Plastic Prints	0%
Harsh Resins	0%
Certified Organic Cotton	100%
Water Based Inks	100%

tsdesigns.com

printing t-shirts for good™

© 2007

Another company in our constellation of sustainability addicts is T.S. Designs over in Burlington. Tom Sineath and Eric Henry have been partners for decades. They are a screen printing company that once made t-shirts for running shoe companies and the like. They were in the textile business, back when North Carolina had a textile industry.

As company after company moved off to the developing world, and t-shirts became less and less expensive, Tom and Eric faced a choice. Lay off North Carolinians and move operations to Malaysia or Honduras, or make a stand. They reached for sustainability to save their company's life. They went into locally made t-shirts, and non-toxic dyes, and they came out with a "Clothing Facts" label that mimicked the food label found on a can of beans at the supermarket. Rather than reporting on the percentage of grams of fat, they reported on the percentage of sweatshop labor.

It was catchy, and it caught some traction. T.S. Designs reinvented itself from a faceless printer of high volume shirts to a "funky little shirt company that was trying to do the right thing." And like Larry's Beans, they went after sustainability on their campus. They put in gardens and rainwater catchments — I believe they were the first to start flushing toilets with rain water — and they put in a solar tracking array and were one of the first to introduce premium parking spaces for hybrid and biodiesel powered vehicles. They have a wind turbine in the side yard, for crying out loud.

Tom is the inventor. Eric is the dreamer. I have a little of each in me. And T.S. Designs is a place I can always go whenever I am looking for hope after a bruising day in the policy layer.

One of my favorite days was the time I drove our short truck over to Burlington to fill up the biodiesel tank in their yard. It was lunch time, and as a "lunch extremist" I filled up the tank and entered the building to find someone I might know for a lunch date. Our friend Melissa works there. She's their sales force. I was doubtful I would see Eric. As the face of the organization he is chronically on the road.

But I bumped into Tom, who had already eaten. He gave me an impromptu tour of the place, showing me his strategy for keeping deer out of the garden, and his methane digester, which was yet another experiment of Dr. Jack Martin. T.S. Design's campus is occasionally a playground for Jack, and you can see vestiges of his science experiments about the place.

If you want to see compost as a heat source for the greenhouse, or a solar cooker large enough to warm a planet, or if you want to see the "run over" remains of flawed concepts gone by, T.S. Designs is a great place to start.

Like so many of us in the DIY sustainable underground, Tom cannot resist the urge to give me a tour. He shows me where his plant wall shades his factory wall, and where his natural wetland exists.

Tom is a pragmatist. Who is proud of his enterprise. He likes to show it off to guys like me.

From the beginning we have been sharing information openly. Occasionally Eric introduces me to a crowd at a ribbon cutting, or a speaking event or some such, and when he does so he more often than not tells the audience that he picked up his first methanol from me when he started making his own biodiesel. To this day, at T.S. Designs, there is a biodiesel cooperative out back that makes its own fuel for its members. We've helped on some design suggestions and provided some analytical support over the years, but the fuel they make out back is different from our fuel, which is dispensed to our Coop members in the front yard.

In 2009 I spoke at T.S. Design's Green Gala. Here is what I said:

Blog

I probably should begin by attempting to define my relationship to T.S. Designs. I work for Piedmont Biofuels, and I think the best description of our relationship is that of fierce competitors for the sustainability limelight.

Sometimes we go first. We pioneer something, or we make something happen, and we grab some headlines, and T.S. Designs calls and asks if we can help them do that too. At which point we pat them on the head, treat them like a little brother, yawn, and give them a hand.

And sometimes they go first. On those occasions we study the subject, figure out how to replicate their efforts, or do it better, and bring it into the world without giving them any credit whatsoever.

And often they just win. When they do, we ask for guidance in order to copy their endeavors, and whenever that happens they are always forthcoming and generous, but they like to add a smidgen of "Wow, the mighty Piedmont needs our help, sure we will help — usually we are following you."

Whenever I am a "sustainability supplicant" to T.S Designs, I can see the sarcasm drip from Eric Henry's text messages.

But I am not supposed to be talking about T.S. Designs. I am supposed to be talking about local economy. And for that I have a favorite T.S. Designs story to tell.

Once a local Pittsboro merchant came out with a "Buy Local" t-shirt. On the front was a pro-Pittsboro message, and on the back was a list of local businesses from which people could procure products and services. I believe Piedmont Biofuels was on the list. I don't think we paid to be there, but we were on the shirt just the same. This t-shirt was not my project.

I first encountered it at Chatham Marketplace, where the shirt's creator approached me with pride to show me the new "Buy Local" t-shirt in town. I don't actually wear t-shirts, but I read his with interest.

And I looked at the label. Made in Honduras.

I handed the shirt back to him and suggested that there is a sustainable t-shirt maker just across the county line in Burlington called T.S. Designs.

And he immediately balked. "Too expensive," was his claim.

I shrugged. I didn't buy his "Buy Local" t-shirt from Honduras, and he eventually vanished from our local economy.

My next tale of cluelessness came from "Wake Up Wednesday," which is a remarkable monthly local business event that occurs in Pittsboro.

Wake Up Wednesday was created in part by Lesley Landis, and it was inspired in part by Becky Anderson, the creator of Handmade in America.

I love Lesley. I love Becky. I love "Wake up Wednesday."

But the last time I was there I paid my entry fee with a PLENTY. That's our local currency. I said, "I'm assuming you take PLENTYs?"

And the woman at the door, who apparently runs our downtown merchant association replied, "I will take it, but I will have to cash it in right away."

By that she meant she would need to convert it into federal reserve notes at our local branch of Capital Bank.

To which I replied, "Why don't you spend it locally on something you need?"

To which she replied, "I need a banner, that I am going to get at Banners.com."

To which I replied, "Why don't you get it from our new sign shop, they make banners, and they would probably appreciate the business."

To which she replied, "I'm sure they are more expensive."

Like the fellow who created the "Buy Local" t-shirt made in Honduras, it was yet another "buy local" organizer who failed to even grasp the concept she was promoting.

Think about it. Wake Up Wednesday buys a banner from the new banner maker; new banner maker contributes to Wake Up Wednesday. It's kinda simple.

I buy from you. You buy from me. We trade amongst ourselves. We keep the dollars inside our community. And voila. The whole community is enriched.

Local economy is easy. Buy your food from your local farmer. Buy your honey from the beekeeper down the street. Buy your t-shirts from your local t-shirt maker, and your banners from your local sign shop, and your books from your local bookstore and on and on and on. And by all means, don't forget to buy your fuel from your local fuel maker.

Buying local is easy. It reduces energy consumption. And that impacts climate change.

I wasn't invited here today to talk about global climate change, but since it is a local economy issue I feel it is warranted.

I'm 47. I have a daughter who is 23. Let's pretend that by some cosmic fluke I make it 47 more years. That means I could see a great-granddaughter on my lap.

Imagine if you will, a great-granddaughter climbing into my lap in 2056.

On our current path our water reservoirs will be empty, and if they have water it will not be fit to drink. Our aquifer will be depleted and our wells will be dry. By the time my great-granddaughter comes along, we will be parched.

On our current trajectory our air will not be suitable for breathing. We will wear respirators and we will stay indoors, filtering our air. Today it is unusual to see a pedestrian wearing a particulate filter, or a SARS mask in an airport. If we do nothing to stop climate change, both will be standard equipment for all of us.

Climate change is the moral imperative of my generation. It is our World War Two. You might say we haven't started fighting yet, but it is time to start. And increasing our participation in our local economy is one way to reduce our carbon footprint. They can be connected.

When my great-granddaughter asks me about the war against climate change, what am I supposed to say? We were going to fight it but it was too expensive? Or am I supposed to say we did nothing?

That's not actually what I am going to say. What I will tell her is that we tried things that failed, and we tried again to discover things that worked. I want to tell her that I fought in the war with everything I had. All my passion, my time, and my money went into the war effort, and battles were won.

I want to tell her about how we won the war against climate change. I want to tell her about how my father served in World War Two. That was his generation's fight.

My generation's fight is with climate change, and I am ready to serve.

My speech went something like that. I gave credit to Chris Turner, the author of *The Geography of Hope*, which has inspired me to get back on my war footing. And when we progressed into questions and answers, we got around to the subtitle of Jared Diamond's *Collapse*, which is subtitled, *How Societies Choose to Fail or Succeed*.

I suggested to the audience that we start the war now, and that we choose to succeed...

❀ ❀ ❀

In the summer of 2009 my daughter Jessalyn was publishing a newsletter for her New York advertising firm, Green Team, and she asked me to contribute a piece on "Change." I should say that in my 28 years of submitting writing to editors for publication, it was a delight to have one of them be my daughter.

Here is what I wrote:

---*blog*---

Agents of Change

The other day I was leaving Community Family Medicine, where I had been for an asthma appointment, when Dr. Holt made a point of coming out to meet me.

"I thought I recognized that voice," he said, "How's our pioneer?"

"I'm good," I replied. "Dr. Butler here was just helping me get some arrows out of my back."

We had a few laughs. I got a prescription for a new inhaler. And all was right in the world.

In our small southern town, I'm known as one of the guys who brought biodiesel to our neck of the woods.... We collect used cooking oil from area restaurants and spin it into fuel and we sell our fuel to a membership community who loves to drive around free of the petroleum grid.

We are in the energy business.

Our company, Piedmont Biofuels, went on to spawn a couple of sustainable farming operations, and we anchored an abandoned industrial park which has become an eco-industrial complex with a bunch of like-minded businesses inside the fence.

These days I'm less interested in the energy balance of our cleaner burning renewable fuel than I am in the change we have created.

To call our membership "awakening consumers" would be a misnomer. They have been wide-awake for a long time, and they completely get it. They understand that by pumping our yellow fuel into their cars and trucks and tractors they are liberating themselves from war, and climate change, and undesirable health effects. They are freeing themselves from little things. Like asthma.

For that they pay a premium. And they go out of their way. And they do it deliberately, and intentionally, in order to be "free" of a centralized top-down fossil energy paradigm that they find oppressive. They are happy to join Piedmont Biofuels, to help us escort them into a low carbon future.

Yet for every consumer who understands our mission, for everyone on our side who "gets it," it feels like there are a thousand others who find our message and us horrifying. Stalwart defenders of the status quo — mechanics and engine makers and cheap fuel loyalists who have a hard time conceiving of how we can possibly exist.

As agents of change we are both heralded and hated.

What I find intriguing is that we are not alone.

Over in Chapel Hill, my friend Tim has run into the same problem. He spent some time in Iceland with renowned architect Bill McDonough (the Cradle to Cradle guy) and together they hatched a plan to build a skyscraper called Greenbridge.

Those of us in the renewable energy space welcomed the news. We loved a built environment that consumed way less energy per square foot than anything else in the region. We applauded when we learned that the investors had forgone residential density in order to accommodate increased daylighting. We saw Greenbridge as a potential model for how humans might exist on earth. Awakening consumers placed deposits, in order to reduce their ecological footprint.

Yet Greenbridge has vocal opponents. Those who want the world to stay the same. Some are a handful of anarchists who run around town sticking up "Fuck Greenbridge" signs. A few twenty-something anarchists are fighting for the status quo with spray paint, while their parents stay silent. Tim describes those who stay silent as North Carolinians who still "go along to get along."

If Greenbridge has a million dollar corner condo on the top floor they are labeled for "million dollar green." Detractors forget to mention the affordable housing that is built into the project — by design — as a study for how humans might live together.

Greenbridge is much larger than Piedmont Biofuels, but folks love to sling mud and arrows at both projects.

It is impossible for me to reflect on this notion without thinking of my brother Glen.

He is in the wind business in Canada, with his one-man company, Sky Generation. When he sold his farm and moved to Lion's Head he broke our family's heart. For years we gathered at his place and planted trees, and we were smug as we watched the forest evolve. But Glen sold the place, moved away, and erected a lone wind turbine on the Bruce Peninsula.

He garnered vast community support, demonstrated the wind energy resource, and managed to land bank financing to build two more. Sky Generation showed a little promise, so he developed a site for six more turbines in Southern Ontario. He too is in the business of energy.

A lot of people believed in Glen, and in his vision of renewable energy. When Bull Frog Power came along, and offered to market his "green electrons," Glen found a partner that worked. Bull Frog has the consumers Glen needs.

Lion's Head is "cottage country," and it is a delight to pull into a place like Harvest Moon Organic Bakery and see the "Powered by Bull Frog Power" stickers on the door. Lots of people on the peninsula "Get it." Lots of people pay a premium for Glen's electricity in order to be free of the human health effects of coal fired and nuclear power plants.

When the "big wind" developers descended on his part of the world, with a plan to put in a hundred more turbines, Glen voluntarily helped organize the landowners and the community to see what a big wind project might look like.

Yet for everyone who signs up for change, it sometimes feels like there are a thousand non-believers. Glen has become a target of the anti-wind energy crowd. Some fellow in Miller Lake is busy buying full-page advertisements in the local paper spouting gibberish about the dangers of electricity of wind. His tagline is "What the Wind Tycoons Don't Tell You."

So Glen, like me, and Tim, gets a turn at the whipping post. All three of us are up against myths, falsehoods, fear, misunderstanding, and the entrenched interests of the status quo. All three of us have just enough hip customers to make our projects succeed. And each of us carries such belief in the low carbon future that we are willing to take risks on its behalf. Clearly the market will have to shift our way.

It's not easy being covered with mud and arrows. My preference would be to sharpen a pine tree down at my shop, heat it to cherry red on the forge, and thrust it into the gelatinous eye of the myopic status quo.

But until then, I guess I will just remain an agent of change. I'll reach for my keyboard, and my inhaler, and keep putting out suggestions for how the market might awake to a different way of being...

When T.S. Designs launched its virtual site tour on its website I was flushed with jealousy and wanted to know how it was done. Eric Henry introduced me to Eric Michel, the big-brained media type who had developed that portion of the site (and who is writing a book on the T.S. Designs story), and they freely shared their code so that I could implement a virtual tour of our eco-industrial park on our site. The reality is that we all take our lead from one another.

We find inspiration where we can get it, and my inspiration is certainly not limited to Larrys Beans, Southern Energy Management, and T.S. Designs. Sometimes something as small as a well-crafted email from Bountiful Backyards will inspire me to take action.

Larry Larson af Larrys Beans and Lyle at the Shakori Grassroots Festival of Music and Dance.

One time when I was sitting at the Coffee Barn at the Shakori Hills Festival of Music and Dance, I bumped into Larry. At the time I was focused on our new worm bins, and Larry and Kevin had one on order. I was transferring my enthusiasm for vermiculture, and Larry was grateful. He said, "It's nice to have someone else lead for a change."

As I reflected on that conversation, I thought about how we all take turns. Southern Energy Management breaks new ground, and we all follow along. Larry's Beans has a breakthrough and we all follow suit (or would like to based on the resources available at the time), and occasionally it is Piedmont Biofuels that is carrying the torch of sustainable practices.

The reason I have focused on these companies is because sustainability is not a sideline. It's not an afterthought. It is at the fore. I often belittle the People-Profit-Planet model — the alleged triple bottom line of sustainability in business — since profits so often carry the day, and planet is often merely lip service to sell more pointless stuff.

My one regret on this front is the time I was addressing an audience of the National Biodiesel Board at the Moscone Center in San Francisco. The speaker that went before me was Kumar Plocher, founder of Yokayo Biofuels. Kumar has long been an inspiration to us on the biodiesel front, and when it comes to making sustainable biodiesel, or perhaps I should say, when it comes to creating community-scale biodiesel, no one in America has more experience than Kumar. He's a hero of mine. And an important figure on our project.

I was stunned to see him in a suit and tie. And I was so disappointed in his People-Planet-Profit speech that I could not help but ridicule the notion, saying things like, "What are we going to do with our big stacks of money when the planet is uninhabitable?"

The companies I admire most, like Yokayo Biofuels, and those from which I draw inspiration, are those who truly put sustainability at the fore.

I also love the Shakori Hills Grassroots Festival of Music and Dance, because they make an effort. But making an effort is different from pushing the envelope. Shakori offers free parking to cars with lots of passengers, and they have arranged a bus loop to Durham to cut down on traffic. And they have a "Solarize Shakori" project underway in which they are attempting to build an array that will make more energy than the festival consumes. They have started rejecting "far away food" vendors in favor of local ones, they run their tractors on our fuel, and they no doubt do a lot of other things that I am not aware of to reduce the footprint of their festival.

But "greening" a festival — or any other business does not provide the same inspiration as having sustainability up front. Shakori inspires me as a project that arose from the landscape as a truly grassroots effort, but they are new to the sustainability movement.

Describing the relationships that exist between companies is complex. While it is certainly that of customer and supplier, it is much deeper than that. It may have a competitive component in that we all take satisfaction from topping one another's efforts, and it certainly is cooperative at its heart. Piedmont Biofuels has longed for a bus for years. Larry's Beans put an eye popping short bus on the road for both coffee deliveries and to shuttle humans around. They win on the bus front. Yet when the bus is struggling, they occasionally tap Rachel for advice, which she freely gives, because she knows the Larry's Beans bus matters.

What we know for sure is that they are not linked by mere money. We are a network of like-minded companies, but unlike the Chamber of Commerce, in which the common bond is simply making money, our common bond is deeper than that.

My brother Jim is the king of networking. He's an expert in business, and is immersed in the world of making money. That's not what this is about. Certainly we all want to be as prosperous as possible, but my ties to Shakori, Southern Energy Management, or Larry's Beans are not rooted in who is raking in the maximum amount of cash.

I like not being alone. From Tim's Greenbridge, in which profits were forgone in exchange for daylighting, to Bountiful Backyard's planting of an edible landscape at the Durham Farmers Market using volunteer labor, to Kevin's rainwater delivery system, everything tends to interlock in a way that inspires me to push on with our own endeavors.

Epilogue

W**RITING A CHRONICLE** like this is fraught with the peril of obsolescence. By the time this book appears on bookstore shelves many new stories will have begun, and many of these stories will need revising. Books of this nature are snapshots in time.

The Plant in springtime. Native, drought-resistant plants attract beneficial pollinators to the surrounding farm.

In February 2010, I took an extended break from the project to go sailing in the Virgin Islands with my brother Glen. It was a much-needed, high-carbon vacation that let me catch up on some reading and let me clear my head.

As an investor in Piedmont Biofuels, Glen has been intimate with our journey, and our struggle for financial viability, and he merely shrugs it off as, "Your problem is the policy layer isn't settled yet."

And he is absolutely right. Biodiesel today is a world of theoretical mandates that go unheeded, subsidies that come and go depending on the year, and grant monies that follow the fashion of the day. It's a challenging space in which to find our business niche. I'm not sure what the ecological equivalent would be — perhaps the mussel which ties itself to a rock and finds a way to survive in the interface between a great pounding ocean and a shore full of predators.

On our journey, Piedmont has sustained many body blows, each of which were substantial enough to take us down.

A high angle view of the Plant from Piedmont Biofarm.

The death of my brother Mark changed the project inexorably. By now we are able to think of our stronger management team in a positive light, but at the time that he died there was very little illuminating the way forward.

The "credit crunch" which followed took many companies with it, as did the great recession of 2008–2009. During that time we learned how to operate without money, executing decisions on a razor's edge and thereby improving our odds at economic sustainability.

Our tank explosion alone would be enough to knock lesser companies out of business. Yet it strengthened ours.

Our spills have also posed major threats.

We have been buffeted by global commodity markets, roughed up by multi-billion-dollar companies, and we have survived. And grown. And even prospered. We never set out to become a case study in resilience, but we are still standing, and still excited about the role we can play escorting North Carolina into the low carbon future which awaits.

Basically we have merely adapted to our ecological niche. By focusing on our waste streams, and defining ourselves through sustainability and community we have successfully found a place where our project can reside in the ever evolving world of human industry.

Bibliography

Anielski, Mark. *Are We Happy Yet?* Alternatives Magazine, 2010.

Bane, Peter, ed. *Permaculture Activist.* 2009.

Cowell, Rebekahi. "Welcome to Zombieland." *Independent Weekly*, 2010.

Darwin, Charles. *The Origin of Species.* W.W. Norton, 2002.

De Blij, Harm. *The Power of Place: Geography, Destiny, and Globalization's Rough Landscape.* Oxford University Press, 2009.

Diamond, Jared. *Collapse: How Societies Choose to Fail or Succeed.* Penguin Group, 2005.

Estill, Lyle. *Biodiesel Power: The Passion, the People, and the Politics of the Next Renewable Fuel.* New Society, 2005.

Estill, Lyle. *Small is Possible: Life in a Local Economy.* New Society, 2008.

Heinberg, Richard. *Power Down: Options and Actions for a Post Carbon World.* New Society, 2004.

Hren, Stephen and Rebekah. *The Carbon Free Home: 36 Remodeling Projects to Help Kick the Fossil-Fuel Habit.* Chelsea Green, 2008.

Hren, Stephen and Rebekah. "From Carbon Free Home to Carbon Free Office." *Huffington Post*, December 8, 2009.

Keillor, Garrison. *A Prairie Home Companion.* National Public Radio.

Margonelli, Lisa. *Oil on the Brain: Adventures from the Pump to the Pipeline.* Random House, 2007.

McDonough, William. *Cradle to Cradle: Remaking the Way We Make Things.* North Point Press, 2002.

Pollan, Michael. *The Omnivore's Dilemma: A Natural History of Four Meals.* The Penguin Press, 2006.

Rushkoff, Douglas. *Life Inc.: How the World Became a Corporation and How to Take It Back.* Random House, 2009.

Schultz, Mark, ed. *Chapel Hill News.* News and Observer, 2009.

Sterne, Laurence. *The Life and Opinions of Tristram Shandy, Gentleman.* Penguin Classics, 1904.

Sustainable World Coalition. *Sustainable World Sourcebook.* Earth Island Institute, 2010.

Turner, Chris. *The Geography of Hope: A Tour of the World We Need.* Random House Canada, 2007.

Wrangham, Richard. *Catching Fire: How Cooking Made Us Human.* Basic Books, 2009.

Index

About the Author

L YLE ESTILL is the president of Piedmont Biofuels in Pittsboro, North Carolina. As such he drives big trucks, and turns valves, and cleans up spills while he thinks about how humans might live differently on this garden planet.

When he is not sucking grease out of metal drums he can be found speaking, lecturing, and giving tours. When he is not obsessing about societal change he can be found gardening, playing chess, raising children, cooking, and watching birds.

His life goal is to become a sailor.

About the photographer

Where Lyle does the words, Tami does the pictures. The two are hopelessly dependent on one another.

Tami has been active in photography for the past twenty years, taking pictures of everything from art to children to industrial design. Her photographs provide stock footage for life in Pittsboro, North Carolina, where they are a mainstay from marketing to memories.

With one eye toward glitter, and another focused on the "fun" part of the human condition, her photographs embellish her community.

She is unclear about her life goal and unsure of whether or not she likes the open sea.

If you have enjoyed *Industrial Evolution,* you might also enjoy other

BOOKS TO BUILD A NEW SOCIETY

Our books provide positive solutions for people who want to
make a difference. We specialize in:

**Sustainable Living • Green Building • Peak Oil
Renewable Energy • Environment & Economy
Natural Building & Appropriate Technology
Progressive Leadership • Resistance and Community
Educational & Parenting Resources**

New Society Publishers

ENVIRONMENTAL BENEFITS STATEMENT

New Society Publishers has chosen to produce this book on recycled paper made
with **100% post consumer waste,** processed chlorine free, and old growth free.
For every 5,000 books printed, New Society saves the following resources:[1]

20	Trees
1,774	Pounds of Solid Waste
1,952	Gallons of Water
2,546	Kilowatt Hours of Electricity
3,225	Pounds of Greenhouse Gases
14	Pounds of HAPs, VOCs, and AOX Combined
5	Cubic Yards of Landfill Space

[1]Environmental benefits are calculated based on research done by the Environmental Defense Fund
and other members of the Paper Task Force who study the environmental impacts of the paper
industry.

For a full list of NSP's titles, please call 1-800-567-6772 or check out our website at:

www.newsociety.com

NEW SOCIETY PUBLISHERS
Deep Green for over 30 years